Cambridge
First Certificate
in English

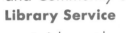

CAMBRIDGE
UNIVERSITY PRESS

PUBLISHED BY THE PRESS SYNDICATE OF THE UNIVERSITY OF CAMBRIDGE
The Pitt Building, Trumpington Street, Cambridge, United Kingdom

CAMBRIDGE UNIVERSITY PRESS
The Edinburgh Building, Cambridge CB2 2RU, UK
40 West 20th Street, New York NY 10011–4211, USA
477 Williamstown Road, Port Melbourne, VIC 3207, Australia
Ruiz de Alarcón 13, 28014 Madrid, Spain
Dock House, The Waterfront, Cape Town 8001, South Africa

http://www.cambridge.org

First published 2003

Printed in the United Kingdom at the University Press, Cambridge

ISBN 0 521 75443 7 Student's Book
ISBN 0 521 75444 5 Student's Book (with answers)
ISBN 0 521 75446 1 Teacher's Book
ISBN 0 521 75447 X Set of 2 Cassettes
ISBN 0 521 75448 8 Set of 2 Audio CDs
ISBN 0 521 75445 3 Self-Study pack

Contents

Introduction

The Cambridge ESOL Main Suite: a five-level system

The University of Cambridge ESOL Examinations has developed a series of examinations with similar characteristics, spanning five levels. Within the series of five levels, the First Certificate in English (FCE) is at Cambridge/ALTE Level 3, Level B2 in the Council of Europe Framework and Level 1 in the UK National Qualifications Framework.

Examination	Cambridge/ALTE Level	Council of Europe Framework Level	UK National Qualifications Framework Level
CPE Certificate of Proficiency in English	Level 5	C2	3
CAE Certificate in Advanced English	Level 4	C1	2
FCE First Certificate in English	Level 3	B2	1
PET Preliminary English Test	Level 2	B1	Entry 3
KET Key English Test	Level 1	A2	Entry 2
YLE Cambridge Young Learners English	Breakthrough Level		

The level of FCE

The First Certificate in English (FCE) offers an intermediate-level qualification for those wishing to use English for professional, social or study purposes. A brief description of FCE level is given below. The description is not a specification for the examination content, but refers to language activities in the real-world, non-examination context. Learners at this level are able to handle the main structures of the language with some confidence, demonstrate knowledge of a wide range of

1

vocabulary and use appropriate communicative strategies in a variety of social situations. Their understanding of spoken language and written texts should go beyond being able to pick out items of factual information, and they should be able to distinguish between main and subsidiary points and between the gist of a text and specific detail. They should be able to produce written texts of various types, showing the ability to develop an argument as well as describe or recount events.

FCE candidates

In 2001, there were approximately 270,000 candidates for FCE throughout the world. Information is collected about the FCE candidates at each session, when candidates fill in a Candidate Information Sheet. Candidates come from a wide range of backgrounds and take the examination for a number of different reasons. The following points summarise the characteristics of the current FCE candidature.

Nationality

FCE is taken by candidates throughout the world in about 100 countries, although the total number of nationalities represented by the candidature is over 150. The majority of these candidates enter for FCE in European and South American countries. Many candidates also take the examination in the UK.

Age

Most candidates (about 75%) are under 25, with the average age being about 21. In some countries the average age is lower (e.g. in Greece it is about 16 years old).

Gender

About 65% of candidates are female.

Employment

Most candidates are students, although there are considerable differences in the proportion of students in different countries.

Exam preparation

A large proportion of candidates (about 85%) undertake a preparatory course before taking the examination; most of these courses last between 8 and 24 weeks.

Reasons for taking FCE

The most frequent reason for candidates wanting the FCE qualification is for work in their own country. Other reasons include work in another country and further study.

Further information

FCE is held each year in March, June and December in 1,900 centres worldwide. Special arrangements are available for disabled candidates. These may include extra time, separate accommodation or equipment, Braille transcription, etc. Consult the Cambridge ESOL Local Secretary in your area for more details.

Copies of the Regulations and details of entry procedure, current fees and further information about this and other Cambridge examinations can be obtained from the Local Secretary for Cambridge ESOL examinations in your area or from:

University of Cambridge
ESOL Examinations
1 Hills Road
Cambridge
CB1 2EU
United Kingdom

Telephone: +44 1223 553355
Fax: +44 1223 460278
e-mail: ESOLHelpdesk@ucles.org.uk
www.CambridgeESOL.org

In some areas this information can also be obtained from the British Council.

FCE content and marking

The structure of FCE: an overview

The FCE examination consists of five papers:

Paper 1	Reading	1 hour 15 minutes
Paper 2	Writing	1 hour 30 minutes
Paper 3	Use of English	1 hour 15 minutes
Paper 4	Listening	40 minutes (approximately)
Paper 5	Speaking	14 minutes

Material used throughout FCE is as far as possible authentic and free of bias, and reflects the international flavour of the examination. The subject matter should not advantage or disadvantage certain groups of candidates, nor should it offend in areas such as religion, politics or sex.

Paper 1   Reading

The FCE Reading paper consists of four parts. Each part consists of a text and a corresponding comprehension task. Part 4 may contain two or more shorter related texts. There is a total of 35 questions. The time allowed to select answers and record them on the answer sheet is one hour fifteen minutes.

Texts

The length of FCE texts varies from 350 words to 700 words, depending on the type of task. The total reading load for the paper is 1,900 to 2,300 words. The texts are intended to cover a range of recently published material and to appear authentic in form, presentation and content.

Texts may be of the following types:

- newspaper and magazine articles
- fiction
- informational material (brochures, guides, manuals)
- advertisements
- correspondence
- messages
- reports

Pictures and other diagrams are used where appropriate to illustrate the text; questions do not focus on visual elements. Some of the vocabulary may be simplified in the texts to keep it within the FCE level but such changes are kept to a minimum.

Test focus

The tasks in the Reading paper test candidates' ability to:

- understand gist and main ideas
- understand detail
- follow text structure
- deduce meaning
- select specific information

Tasks

There are 35 questions on the Reading paper. Each text is accompanied by a set of questions as follows:

Part	Task	Number of Questions	Task Format
1	Multiple matching	6 or 7	Candidates must match headings or summary sentences to paragraphs of the text.
2	Multiple choice	7 or 8	Candidates must answer multiple-choice questions based on the text.
3	Gapped text	6 or 7	Candidates must select appropriate paragraphs or sentences that have been removed from the text and jumbled.
4	Multiple matching	13 to 15	Candidates must locate information in the text or texts.

Multiple-choice and gapped-text questions follow the text; multiple-matching questions precede the text.

The language level of the instructions and individual questions is within the range of FCE.

Marks

Candidates record their answers by shading the correct lozenges on a separate answer sheet.

Two marks are given for each correct answer in **Parts 1, 2** and **3** and one mark is given for each correct answer in **Part 4**. The total score is then weighted to 40 marks for the whole Reading paper.

Marking

The Reading paper is directly scanned by computer.

Paper 2   Writing

The FCE Writing paper requires candidates to carry out two tasks: a compulsory task in **Part 1** and one from a choice of four questions in **Part 2**. Candidates are expected to write 120–180 words for each task, making a total overall word length of 240–360 words across the two tasks. The time allowed to complete the two tasks is one hour thirty minutes. There is an optional question on background reading texts in **Part 2**.

Test focus

Part 1 is a compulsory task in which candidates have to produce a transactional letter. Information is given about a specific situation through a combination of text and notes, sometimes supported by illustrations or diagrams. In **Part 2** there is a choice of four tasks from which candidates choose one. All of the questions specify why the piece is to be written and who the piece is to be written for.

    Parts 1 and **2** carry equal marks.

Tasks

In **Part 1**, the language of the reading input and rubric is well within the level expected of FCE candidates. Candidates are required to write a transactional letter in an appropriate style. The purpose of the letter and the addressee are clearly explained in the rubric. In order to complete the task successfully, candidates need to use the input provided in an appropriate way, expanding on the points given by using a range of structures and vocabulary.

In **Part 2**, candidates are expected to write one of the following:

- an article
- an informal/non-transactional letter
- a discursive composition
- a short story
- a report
- a letter of application

There is an optional task (question 5) on background reading texts in **Part 2**. There are two alternatives in question 5 and candidates may select one of these based on their reading of the set texts. The list of set texts is published by Cambridge ESOL in the Examination Regulations. Each text normally remains on the list for two years.

Assessment

An impression mark is awarded to each task; examiners use band descriptors similar to the ones on page 7 to assess how well the task has been realised.

    The **general impression mark scheme** is used in conjunction with a **task-specific mark scheme,** which focuses on criteria specific to each particular task. This summarises the content, organisation and cohesion, range of structures and vocabulary, register and format, and target reader indicated in the task.

    American usage and spelling is acceptable; marks are not specifically deducted for spelling errors, although a number of errors which interfere with communication will affect the assessment.

GENERAL MARK SCHEME

5	Full realisation of the task set. • All content points included with appropriate expansion. • Wide range of structure and vocabulary within the task set. • Minimal errors, perhaps due to ambition; well-developed control of language. • Ideas effectively organised, with a variety of linking devices. • Register and format consistently appropriate to purpose and audience. Fully achieves the desired effect on the target reader.
4	Good realisation of the task set. • All major content points included: possibly one or two minor omissions. • Good range of structure and vocabulary within the task set. • Generally accurate, errors occur mainly when attempting more complex language. • Ideas clearly organised, with suitable linking devices. • Register and format on the whole appropriate to purpose and audience. Achieves the desired effect on the target reader.
3	Reasonable achievement of the task set. • All major content points included; some minor omissions. • Adequate range of structure and vocabulary, which fulfils the requirements of the task. • A number of errors may be present, but they do not impede communication. • Ideas inadequately organised, with simple linking devices. • Reasonable, if not always successful, attempt at register and format appropriate to purpose and audience. Achieves, on the whole, the desired effect on the target reader.
2	Task set attempted but not adequately achieved. • Some major content points inadequately covered or omitted, and/or some irrelevant material. • Limited range of structure and vocabulary. • A number of errors, which distract the reader and may obscure communication at times. • Ideas inadequately organised; linking devices rarely used. • Unsuccessful/inconsistent attempts at appropriate register and format. Message not clearly communicated to the target reader.
1	Poor attempt at the task set. • Notable content omissions and/or considerable irrelevance, possibly due to misinterpretation of the task set. • Narrow range of vocabulary and structure. • Frequent errors which obscure communication; little evidence of language control. • Lack of organisation or linking devices. • Little or no awareness of appropriate register and format. Very negative effect on the target reader.
0	Achieves nothing: too little language for assessment (fewer than 50 words) or totally irrelevant or totally illegible.

All these comments should be interpreted at FCE level, and referred to in conjunction with a task-specific mark scheme.

Marking

The panel of examiners is divided into small teams, each with a very experienced examiner as Team Leader. The Principal Examiner guides and monitors the marking process. This begins with a meeting of the Principal Examiner and the Team Leaders. This is held immediately after the examination and begins the process of establishing a common standard of assessment by the selection of sample scripts for all five questions in Paper 2. Sample scripts are chosen to demonstrate the range of responses and different levels of competence, and a **task-specific mark scheme** is finalised for each individual question on the paper. The accuracy of language, including spelling and punctuation, is assessed on the **general impression scale** for all tasks. Markers discuss these mark schemes and refer to them regularly while they are working. A rigorous process of co-ordination and checking is carried out before and throughout the marking process.

Paper 3   Use of English

The FCE Use of English paper contains five parts. There is a total of 65 questions. The time allowed for completion of all five parts, including answer sheet completion, is one hour fifteen minutes.

Test focus

This paper tests the ability of candidates to apply their knowledge of the language system. **Part 1** emphasises vocabulary; **Parts 2** and **3** focus on both grammar and vocabulary; **Part 4** emphasises grammar and **Part 5** focuses closely on grammar.

Tasks

There are 65 questions in the Use of English paper. Each part of the paper contains a set of questions as follows:

Part 1

A cloze text of approximately 200 words, modified to place emphasis on lexical items, with 15 four-option multiple-choice items.

Part 2

An open cloze text of approximately 200 words, modified to place emphasis on structural words. The text contains 15 gaps to be completed by the candidate. There may be a small number of lexico-grammatical items.

Part 3

A set of ten sentences, each accompanied by a 'key' word and a gapped reformulation of the initial sentence. Candidates are required to complete the gapped sentence, using the key word, so that it has a similar meaning to the prompt sentence.

Part 4

A text of approximately 200 words which contains 15 lines (plus two example lines). Some lines of the text are correct, other lines contain an extra incorrect word, which candidates are required to identify. No line contains more than one error.

Part 5

A text of approximately 150 words which contains ten gaps. Each gap corresponds to a word. The 'stems' of the missing words are given beside the text and must be transformed to provide the missing words.

Marks

One mark is given for each correct answer in **Parts 1, 2, 4 and 5**. For **Part 3**, candidates are awarded a mark of 2, 1 or 0 for each question according to the accuracy of their response. Correct spelling is required in **Parts 2, 3, 4 and 5**. The total mark is subsequently weighted to 40.

Marking

Part 1 of the Use of English paper is directly scanned by computer. The other parts of the paper are marked under the supervision of a co-ordinating examiner. A mark scheme is drawn up in the light of pre-testing. This is adjusted at the beginning of the marking procedure to take account of actual candidate performance and then finalised. All scripts are double-marked. Question papers may be scrutinised during the marking if there is any doubt about candidate responses on the answer sheets.

Paper 4   Listening

The Listening paper is divided into four parts and is approximately 40 minutes in length. Each part contains a recorded text or texts and corresponding comprehension tasks. There is a total of 30 questions in the Listening paper. Each text is heard twice.

Recordings contain a variety of accents corresponding to standard variants of English native-speaker accent, and to English non-native speaker accents that approximate to the norms of native-speaker accents. Background sounds may be included before speaking begins, to provide contextual information.

The instructions for each task are heard and read by the candidate. They give the general context for the input and explain the task.

Candidates are advised to write their answers on the question paper while listening. Five minutes are allowed at the end of the test for candidates to transfer their answers onto an answer sheet.

You will need to pause your audio CD before Parts 2, 3 and 4, and at the end of the test. The length of the pauses is announced to you. The audio cassettes, however, contain all pauses between parts, and only need to be paused for five minutes at the end of the test.

Texts

Different text types appropriate to the particular test focus are used in each part of the paper. They may be any of the following types:

Monologues:
- answerphone/freephone messages
- commentaries
- documentaries/features
- instructions
- lectures
- news
- public announcements
- publicity/advertisements
- reports
- speeches
- stories/anecdotes
- talks

Interacting speakers:
- chats
- conversations
- discussions
- interviews
- quizzes
- radio plays
- transactions

Part 1 consists of eight short, unrelated extracts of approximately 30 seconds which may be in the form of monologues or conversations. **Part 2** is a monologue or text involving interacting speakers and lasts approximately 3 minutes. **Part 3** consists of five short related pieces, each with a different speaker, of approximately 30 seconds each. **Part 4** is also a monologue or text involving interacting speakers and lasts approximately 3 minutes.

Test focus

The tasks in the Listening paper test candidates' ability to understand:

Parts 1 and 3

gist, main points, function, location, roles and relationships, mood, attitude, intention, feeling or opinion.

Parts 2 and 4

gist, main points, detail or specific information, or deduce meaning.

Tasks

Each listening text is accompanied by a set of questions as follows:

Part	Task	Number of questions
1	Multiple choice	8
2	Note taking, blank filling, sentence completion	10
3	Multiple matching	5
4	Selection from 2 or 3 possible answers	7

In Part 4, questions may have two alternatives or three, e.g. multiple choice, matching and true/false.

Marks

One mark is given for each correct answer. The total is weighted to give a mark out of 40 for the paper. In Part 2 minor spelling errors are allowed, provided that the candidate's intention is clear. Occasionally candidates are asked to write a word which has been dictated letter-by-letter. This must be spelt correctly.

For security reasons, several versions of the Listening paper are used at each administration of the examination. Before grading, the performance of the candidates in each of the versions is compared and marks adjusted to compensate for any imbalance in levels of difficulty.

Marking

Part 1 and **Part 3** of the Listening paper are directly scanned by computer. The other parts of the paper are marked under the supervision of a co-ordinating examiner. A mark scheme for each version of the Listening paper is drawn up in the light of pre-testing. This is adjusted at the beginning of the marking procedure to take account of actual candidate performance, and then finalised. All scripts are double-marked. Question papers may be scrutinised during the marking if there is any doubt about candidates' responses on the answer sheets.

Paper 5 Speaking test

The FCE Speaking test is conducted by two examiners (an interlocutor who will conduct the test and speak to the candidates, and an assessor who will just listen to the candidates) with pairs of candidates. The test takes fourteen minutes for each pair of candidates and is divided into four parts:

Part 1 Interview
Part 2 Individual long turn
Part 3 Two-way collaborative task
Part 4 Three-way discussion

A pair of colour photographs is provided for each candidate as the visual prompts for **Part 2**, together with a verbal rubric. The prompts for **Part 3** may be in the form of photographs, line drawings, diagrams, etc., together with a verbal rubric. **Parts 1** and **4** do not require visual prompts.

Test focus

The tasks in the Speaking test require candidates to interact in conversational English in a range of contexts. Candidates demonstrate their ability to do this through appropriate control of grammar and vocabulary, discourse management, pronunciation and interactive communication.

Tasks include different interaction patterns (examiner to candidate, candidate to candidate), different discourse types (short turn, long turn, etc.), and focus on different features, such as comparing and contrasting, exchanging information, stating and supporting an opinion, agreeing and disagreeing, expressing certainty and uncertainty, initiating and responding, collaborating, and turn-taking.

Tasks

The purpose of **Part 1** ('interview': three minutes) is to test general interactional and social language.

In this part of the test, candidates respond to direct questions asked by the interlocutor. Candidates are expected to expand on their responses, talking about present circumstances, past experiences and future plans.

The purpose of **Part 2** ('individual long turn': one minute per candidate) is to elicit a sample of transactional language from each candidate.

In **Part 2** each candidate is given the opportunity to talk without interruption for one minute. Candidates demonstrate their ability to organise their language and ideas with an appropriate use of grammar and vocabulary. Each candidate gives information and expresses opinions through comparing and contrasting two colour photographs.

The purpose of **Part 3** ('collaborative task': approximately three minutes) is to elicit short transactional turns from each candidate by engaging both of them in the same problem-solving activity.

The tasks are designed to give candidates the opportunity to demonstrate their range of language; the metalanguage of the exchange is as much a part of the test as the utterances directly connected with the prompt. All **Part 3** tasks are shared; candidates are encouraged to talk together, without the interlocutor, and should be able to express and justify their own views, invite the opinions and ideas of their partner and negotiate a decision.

The purpose of **Part 4** ('three-way discussion': approximately four minutes) is to elicit a further sample of speech from the candidates by allowing them to participate in a wider discussion with the interlocutor of the issues raised in **Part 3**.

At the end of the Speaking test, candidates are thanked for attending but are given no indication of their level of achievement.

NB If there is an uneven number of candidates at a session, the last three candidates will be examined together.

Assessment

Candidates are assessed on their own individual performance and not in relation to each other, according to the following four analytical criteria: grammar and vocabulary, discourse management, pronunciation and interactive communication. These criteria are interpreted at FCE level. Assessment is based on performance in the whole test and not in particular parts of the test.

Both examiners assess the candidates. The assessor applies detailed, analytical scales, and the interlocutor applies a global achievement scale, which is based on the analytical scales.

FCE typical minimum adequate performance

Although there are some inaccuracies, grammar and vocabulary are sufficiently accurate in dealing with the tasks. Mostly coherent, with some extended discourse. Can generally be understood. Able to maintain the interaction and deal with the tasks without major prompting.

Analytical scales

Grammar and vocabulary

This refers to the accurate and appropriate use of grammatical forms and vocabulary. It also includes the range of both grammatical forms and vocabulary. Performance is viewed in terms of the overall effectiveness of the language used.

Discourse management

This refers to the coherence, extent and relevance of each candidate's individual contribution. In this scale the candidate's ability to maintain a coherent flow of language is assessed, either within a single utterance or a string of utterances. Also assessed here is how relevant the contributions are to what has gone before.

Pronunciation

This refers to the candidate's ability to produce comprehensible utterances to fulfil the task requirements. This includes stress, rhythm and intonation as well as individual sounds. Examiners put themselves in the position of the non-EFL specialist and assess the overall impact of the pronunciation and the degree of effort required to understand the candidate.

Interactive communication

This refers to the candidate's ability to use language to achieve meaningful communication. This includes initiating and responding without undue hesitation, the ability to use interactive strategies to maintain or repair communication, and sensitivity to the norms of turn taking.

Global achievement scale

This refers to the candidate's overall performance throughout the test.

Oral Examiners are trained in conducting the FCE Speaking test and applying the assessment criteria at initial training sessions. At these sessions, Oral Examiners conduct tests with volunteer candidates, and mark video sample tests, which are selected to demonstrate a range of levels of competence. After initial training, Oral Examiners attend annual co-ordination sessions to maintain standardisation of marking.

In the majority of countries in which the FCE examination is taken, Oral Examiners are assigned to teams which are led by Team Leaders. Team Leaders give advice and support and also monitor Oral Examiners on a regular basis during live tests. Senior Team Leaders, to whom Team Leaders are responsible, are appointed by Cambridge ESOL to manage the professional aspects of the Speaking tests. Senior Team Leaders attend annual conferences in the UK to co-ordinate the development of the Team Leader system world-wide.

Marks

Marks for each scale are awarded out of five: the assessor's marks are weighted singly and the interlocutor's mark is double-weighted. Marks for the Speaking test are subsequently weighted to produce a final mark out of 40.

Grading and results

Grading takes place once all scripts have been returned to Cambridge ESOL and marking is complete. This is approximately six weeks after the examination.

Grading

The five FCE papers total 200 marks after weighting. Each paper is weighted to 40 marks.

A candidate's overall FCE grade is based on the total score gained by the candidate in all five papers. It is not necessary to achieve a satisfactory level in all five papers in order to pass the examination.

The overall grade boundaries (A, B, C, D and E) are set according to the following information:

- statistics on the candidature
- statistics on the overall candidate performance
- statistics on individual items, for those parts of the examination for which this is appropriate (Papers 1, 3 and 4)
- advice, based on the performance of candidates, and recommendations of examiners, where this is relevant (Papers 2 and 5)
- comparison with statistics from previous years' examination performance and candidature.

Special consideration

Special consideration can be given to candidates affected by adverse circumstances immediately before or during an examination. Examples of acceptable reasons for giving special consideration include illness and bereavement. All applications for special consideration must be made through the centre as soon as posssible after the examination affected.

Irregular conduct

The cases of candidates who are suspected of copying, collusion or breaking the examination regulations in some other way will be considered by the Cambridge ESOL Malpractice Committee. Results may be withheld because further investigation is needed or because of infringement of the regulations.

Results

Results are reported as three passing grades (A, B and C) and two failing grades (D and E). The minimum successful performance which a candidate typically requires in order to achieve a grade C corresponds to about 60% of the total marks. Statements of Results are sent out to all candidates and include a graphical display of the candidate's performance in each paper. These are shown against the scale Exceptional – Good – Borderline – Weak and show the candidate's relative performance in each paper.

Notification of results

Statements of Results are issued through centres approximately two months after the examination has been taken.

Certificates are issued about six weeks after the issue of Statements of Results. Enquiries about results may be made through Local Secretaries, within a month of the issue of Statements of Results.

Paper 2 sample answers and examiner's comments

The following pieces of writing have been selected from students' answers. The samples relate to tasks in Tests 1–4 of the Student's Book. Explanatory notes have been added to show how the bands have been arrived at. The comments should be read in conjunction with the task-specific mark schemes included in the Keys.

Sample A (Test 1, Question 2 – Composition)

> In the past, young people used to wear their parents clothes, so that they would look like if they were older. The truth is, that nowadays, young people, always want to dress differently from their parents.
>
> It seems that to them, that their parents' clothes are 'old-fashioned' and are worn only by the 'old people'. These suits of the young men's fathers, look as they say, like if they were going to a funeral and these dresses of the young women's mothers look like if they were made 'in the wild west'.
>
> And if young people don't wear clothes like their parents', what kind of clothes do they wear and why? Nowadays, young people have a tendency to wear informal clothes, especially really large jeans and T-shirts. The clothes that young men wear don't differ a lot from the young women's. The only exception is, that young women tend to wear really tight trousers and blouses. In my opinion, they want to wear these clothes in order to make a revolution, as they are recieving a lot of pressure from their parents.
>
> In conclusion, young people always want to dress differently from their parents and that's what they really do.

Comments

Content
Good realisation of the task.

Accuracy
Good – errors due to ambition – some repeated errors.

Range
Good range of vocabulary and structure.

Organisation and cohesion
Clear paragraphing; some linking.

Appropriacy of register and format
Consistently appropriate.

Target reader
Would be informed.

Band: 4

Sample B (Test 1, Question 4 – Report)

> To: Mr George Luke, director of the company "Tours"
> From:
> Date: 2nd December 2002
> Subject: One-day sightseeing tour in Paris
>
> <u>Introduction</u>
> As requested, this report is to assess what visitors can see in Paris.
>
> General Information – Facilities
> Paris is the capital of France and is situated in the north of the country. It can be easily reached by plane from many cities of Europe, such as Athens, London, Madrid and Berlin, as well as of New York in USA. The ways of transport in the city are plenty: underground railway (metro), train, bus or taxi.
>
> <u>Interesting Sights</u>
> The city of Paris offers very much to see. Some very interesting places that could be visited are the following: the Sacré Coeur Cathedral in the north of the town, the Notre-Dame, in the certre of Paris, as well as the Tour Eiffel, the well known, huge building. What else could be done is a walk at the avenue of Champs-Elysées and shopping at Galleries Lafayette.
>
> <u>Conclusion</u>
> My personal opinion is that Paris is the most beautiful town and I would strongly recommend to visit it.

Comments

Content
All content points adequately covered.

Accuracy
Generally accurate.

Range
Some evidence of range.

Organisation and cohesion
Clearly organised with good cohesion.

Appropriacy of register and format
Good report format.

Target reader
Would be informed.

Band: 3

Sample C (Test 2, Question 1 – Letter)

Dear Peter,

Thank you very much for your letter. It's been 6 months since our last meeting. A long time, isn't it?

Anyway, of course I have some ideas for Anna's birthday party. Your first suggestion about the Majestic Hotel sounds really good, but what about the price? I'm not sure whether it's too expensive or not.

I think we should order a birthday cake and her favourite food, Italian. That shouldn't be a problem to get.

Well, don't bother because of her present. Anna enjoys travelling, so I think it would be a good idea to give her a trip, which she can choose. Your thought about a watch isn't bad but Anna has got a new one recently.

Anyway, I've bad news for you because I'm very busy the day before the party. So, I can't help you with the preparations. I'm very sorry! I hope you'll find someone else giving you a hand. Maybe Brian.

My suggestion for a special party is that we should organise a Karaoke party. I remember how much she enjoyed the last visit in the Karaoke Bar. That will be a great surprise for Anna.

So, please let me know your decision.

Love,

Comments

Content
All points covered with good expansion.

Accuracy
Very accurate.

Range
Good range with natural tone.

Organisation and cohesion
Well organised and linked.

Appropriacy of register and format
Very appropriate and natural.

Target reader
A convincing letter which informs the target reader.

Band: 5

Sample D (Test 2, Question 2 – Composition)

> I am a egologist person and me and my family take care of environment and so we use public transport. Nowadays, there is a lot of pollution and we have a lot of enviroment problem like greenhouse effect ozone hole. The car is one of the enviroment problems.
>
> Almost all people use car because is more convenient. Why? Because when we need move we don't have to wait the public transport, we don't have to change bus or train. But there are a lot of advantages to take public transport. First of all, it is four our future, less pollution!
>
> Sometimes the public transport are quickly than car, during the travel you can read, sleep, speak with other people. If we take a special card is not so expansive and is less dangerous for the accident.
>
> Disadvantages for the car: the fuel is expansive, a lot of traffic and a lot of danger in the street.
>
> My slogan is less car, less pollution, better life.
>
> Finally, I think in the future we will use more the public transport than the car.

Comments

Content
Good range of appropriate vocabulary.

Accuracy
Frequent errors, sometimes basic.

Range
Ambitious but unsuccessful.

Organisation and cohesion
Disjointed in parts.

Appropriacy of register and format
Suitably neutral register but poor linking.

Target reader
Would understand the message but be distracted by the number of errors.

Band: 2

Sample E (Test 3, Question 1 – Letter)

Dear Donovan

How are you? I hope everything will be all right. If I were you I would go to Castle and lake Trips. It's really nice for a day trip. I went there and it was fantastic.

The departures can be 8 am or 10 a.m. daily but I recomend you at 8 am because there are less people and it's better.

The first stop is at Bourne Castle. There is a beatiful Castle and is important to get a guide tour because they will explain to everybody the Castle's history. After the lunch. You can choose take a picnic instead of a restaurant. It's cheaper. During the afternoon you will go to a beautiful lake where you can play water sports like water-motorcycles. It's really funny! The prices are good and also you can get reductions for groups, minimum 15 people.

I hope this information will be enought for you to consider this trip.

Best wishes

Comments

Content
All points covered.

Accuracy
A number of non-impeding errors.

Range
Adequate.

Organisation and cohesion
Adequate; some reasonable linking.

Appropriacy of register and format
Appropriate.

Target reader
Would be informed.

Band: 3

Sample F (Test 3, Question 4 – Article)

<u>Could you live without television for a week?</u>

That's a good question! It seems very easy just to turn off the TV set and spend your time better. But you have to realise that you must find something instead of watching of TV. I think before you start your first week without TV you must plan your activity. You will see how many things you can do during your new free time. You can for example do something for your health and fitness – you can go swimming, play tennis or go cycling. You can meet your friends, call parents or just do your room. You will be able to read more books or find new hobby. You will see that life is not just TV! I tried to live without television and now I enjoy my life much better. So don't think too long – try! I promise you will not come back to your old, boring black box!

Comments

Content
Good realisation of the task.

Accuracy
Minimal errors.

Range
Good range within the task set; some repetition.

Organisation and cohesion
Appropriate to article format.

Appropriacy of register and format
Appropriate.

Target reader
Achieves the desired effect on the target reader.

Band: 4

Sample G (Test 4, Question 4 – Story)

It was dangerous, but I knew I had to do it. It was a new challenge and not only for me but for everyone there.
Nobody thought I was capable of doing it.
I wasn't sure of what to do, and the pressure of everyone watching me was driving me mad.

Finally, I managed to move my right foot closer to the edge. I could listen the crowd shouting 'to go'. That was my only chance. Only few more seconds, otherwise my time would be over.

I didn't even think of looking down. I was already paralysed, and that wouldn't help me at all.

Then, by some 'strange power' my left foot was moving and I wanted to stop it, but it was too difficult.

The clock was running tic tac. And suddenly everything stopped. I felt an enormous peace. Somehow I managed to jump out of the airplane and I was flying!

Those minutes, up in the air, feeling the wind in my face, were fantastic. And then I was terrified when I couldn't open the parachute! Fortunately, I wasn't alone.

Comments

Content
Good, interesting and dramatic storyline clearly linked to the prompt sentence.

Accuracy
Minimal errors.

Range
Very good use of narrative with a wide range of structure and vocabulary.

Organisation and cohesion
Well organised but over-paragraphed.

Appropriacy of register and format
Appropriate use of narrative technique for suspense.

Target reader
Would enjoy the story.

Band: 5

Sample H (Test 4, Question 5b – Set text, letter)

> Dear friend,
>
> I am writing to you because I would like you to tell you my opinions about 'The old Man and the Sea'. It was the last book I read. I know you want to know if this book would be a suitable present for you cousin's 15 birthday.
>
> Well! to be honest. I think it is not good because the book is quite boring. It was difficulted to understand for me and what is more it has 250 pages. The story is about a man, who fith and speak with the sea. The sea has a big waves and this man want to survive, but he can't. The sea, who can speak with him, it said for example: 'be careful with my deep waters, you can died'.
>
> You know, the book is quite scared, but I think you can chose othe thing more nice. Besides that, your cousin in young, maybe she would prefer something to wear.
>
> Well! Now I'm going out. I hope my advices help you. I'm looking forward to hear from you in the next few days.
>
> Kisses from

Comments

Content
Task attempted but not adequately achieved. Some reference to the story is made, but there is no real evidence of accurate knowledge about the book. The rest of the task is adequately covered.

Accuracy
Some distracting errors.

Range
Adequate.

Organisation and cohesion
Adequate.

Appropriacy of register and format
Good for an informal letter.

Target reader
Would know the writer's opinion about the present, but would not have enough information about the book.

Band: 2

Paper 5 frames

Test 1

Note: In the examination, there will be both an assessor and an interlocutor in the room.

The visual material for **Test 1** appears on pages C1–C4 of the Student's Book.

Part 1   (3 minutes)

Interlocutor: Good morning/afternoon/evening. My name is .... and this is my colleague, ... He/she is just going to listen to us.

And your names are ... ?

Can I have your mark sheets, please?

Thank you.

First of all, we'd like to know something about you, so I'm going to ask you some questions about yourselves.

EITHER (non-UK-based candidates)   OR   (UK-based candidates)

(Candidate A), do you live in .... ?   Where are you from, *(Candidate A)*?
(name of town where examination is being held)
And you, *(Candidate B)*?   And you, *(Candidate B)*?

- What do you like about living *(here / name of candidate's home town)*?
- And what about you, *(Candidate A/B)*?

(Select one or more questions from any of the following categories as appropriate.)

Home and family
- Is there anything you dislike about living in this area?
- Where do you think you'll be this time next year?
- Tell me something about your family.
- What would you like to change about your home?

Daily life and special occasions
- Tell me about your friends.
- Do you have any plans for next weekend?
- Do you normally celebrate special occasions with friends or family? (Why?)
- What did you do on your last birthday?
- What's the next special occasion you're going to celebrate?

Work/education
- What do you do in *(candidate's home town)*, do you work or study?

EITHER (if candidate is already working)
- What do you do?
- What do you like most about your job?
- What do you think you'll be doing in five years' time?

OR *(if candidate is still studying)*
- What subjects are you studying at the moment?
- What do you enjoy about *(one of the subjects named by the candidate)*?
- Are you looking forward to leaving school/college? Why (not)?
- What kind of job are you hoping to do in the future?

Health
- How much exercise do you do?
- How easy do you think it is to keep fit and healthy? Why?
- Do you think people are too interested in keeping fit today?

Interests
- What do you like to do in your free time?
- Do you have enough time to do all the things you enjoy?
- How often do you go to the cinema? *(If they go)* Have you seen any good films recently?
- How have your interests changed in the last few years?
- If you could choose to do something new, what would it be? Why?

Holidays
- Where did you go for your last holiday? Did you enjoy it?
- What kind of things do you like doing on holiday?
- How important is it to have good weather while you're on holiday?
- Are you planning to go anywhere special soon?

Part 2 (4 minutes)

Interlocutor:	Now, I'd like each of you to talk on your own for about a minute.
	I'm going to give each of you two different photographs and I'd like you to talk about them. *(Candidate A)*, here are your two photographs. They show teachers and children.
	Indicate pictures 1A and 1B on page C1 of the Student's Book to Candidate A.
	Please let *(Candidate B)* see them.
	(Candidate B), I'll give you your photographs in a minute.
	(Candidate A), I'd like you to compare and contrast these photographs, and say how important it is to have a teacher in each situation.
	Remember, you have only about a minute for this, so don't worry if I interrupt you. All right?
Candidate A:	[*One minute.*]
Interlocutor:	Thank you.
	(Candidate B), would you like to teach children?
Candidate B:	[*Approximately twenty seconds.*]
Interlocutor:	Thank you.

Now, *(Candidate B)*, here are your two photographs. They show places where people live. Please let *(Candidate A)* have a look at them.

Indicate pictures 1C and 1D on page C4 of the Student's Book to Candidate B.

I'd like you to compare and contrast these photographs, and say what you think it would be like to live and work in places like these.

Remember, *(Candidate B)*, you have only about a minute for this, so don't worry if I interrupt you. All right?

Candidate B: [*One minute.*]

Interlocutor: Thank you.

    (Candidate A), where would you prefer to live?

Candidate A: [*Approximately twenty seconds.*]

Interlocutor: Thank you.

Part 3   (approximately 3 minutes)

Interlocutor: Now, I'd like you to talk about something together for about three minutes. I'm just going to listen.

    Here are some pictures which show things that can make a difference to a holiday.

    Indicate the set of pictures 1E on pages C2–C3 of the Student's Book to the candidates.

    First, talk to each other about the difference these things can make to a holiday. Then decide which two are the most important.

    You have only about three minutes for this. So, once again, don't worry if I stop you, and please speak so that we can hear you. All right?

Candidates
A & B: [*Three minutes.*]

Interlocutor: Thank you.

Part 4   (approximately 4 minutes)

Interlocutor: *Select any of the following questions as appropriate.*

- Why do you think we need holidays?
- Do you prefer to plan your holiday or to go at the last minute?
- How important is it to experience something new when you go on holiday?
- What would you find enjoyable about a holiday in a large city?
- How does the weather affect holidays in your country?
- What is the most popular outdoor activity in your area?

Thank you. That is the end of the test.

Test 2

Note: In the examination, there will be both an assessor and an interlocutor in the room.

The visual material for **Test 2** appears on pages C5–C8 of the Student's Book.

Part 1   (3 minutes)

Interlocutor: Good morning/afternoon/evening. My name is .... and this is my colleague, ... He/she is just going to listen to us.

And your names are ... ?

Could I have your mark sheets, please?

Thank you.

First of all, we'd like to know something about you, so I'm going to ask you some questions about yourselves.

EITHER (non-UK-based candidates) OR   *(UK-based candidates)*

(Candidate A), do you live in .... ?   Where are you from, *(Candidate A)*?
(name of town where examination is being held)
And you, *(Candidate B)*?   And you, *(Candidate B)*?

- What do you like about living *(here / name of candidate's home town)*?
- And what about you, *(Candidate A/B)*?

(Select one or more questions from any of the following categories as appropriate.)

Home and family
- Is there anything you dislike about living in this area?
- Where do you think you'll be this time next year?
- Tell me something about your family.
- What would you like to change about your home?

Daily life and special occasions
- Tell me about your friends.
- Do you have any plans for next weekend?
- Do you normally celebrate special occasions with friends or family? (Why?)
- What did you do on your last birthday?
- What's the next special occasion you're going to celebrate?

Work/education
- What do you do in *(candidate's home town)*, do you work or study?

EITHER (if candidate is already working)
- What do you do?
- What do you like most about your job?
- What do you think you'll be doing in five years' time?

OR (if candidate is still studying)
- What subjects are you studying at the moment?
- What do you enjoy about *(one of the subjects named by the candidate)*?

- Are you looking forward to leaving school/college? Why (not)?
- What kind of job are you hoping to do in the future?

Health
- How much exercise do you do?
- How easy do you think it is to keep fit and healthy? Why?
- Do you think people are too interested in keeping fit today?

Interests
- What do you like to do in your free time?
- Do you have enough time to do all the things you enjoy?
- How often do you go to the cinema? *(If they go)* Have you seen any good films recently?
- How have your interests changed in the last few years?
- If you could choose to do something new, what would it be? Why?

Holidays
- Where did you go for your last holiday? Did you enjoy it?
- What kind of things do you like doing on holiday?
- How important is it to have good weather while you're on holiday?
- Are you planning to go anywhere special soon?

Part 2   (4 minutes)

Interlocutor: Now, I'd like each of you to talk on your own for about a minute.

I'm going to give each of you two different photographs and I'd like you to talk about them. *(Candidate A)*, here are your two photographs. They show people doing different jobs.

Indicate pictures 2A and 2B on page C5 of the Student's Book to Candidate A.

Please let *(Candidate B)* see them.

(Candidate B), I'll give you your photographs in a minute.

(Candidate A), I'd like you to compare and contrast these photographs, and say what you think is difficult about these jobs.

Remember, you have only about a minute for this, so don't worry if I interrupt you. All right?

Candidate A: [*One minute.*]

Interlocutor: Thank you.

(Candidate B), would you like to do either of these jobs?

Candidate B: [*Approximately twenty seconds.*]

Interlocutor: Thank you.

Now, *(Candidate B)*, here are your two photographs. They show different people using the telephone. Please let *(Candidate A)* have a look at them.

Indicate pictures 2C and 2D on page C8 of the Student's Book to Candidate B.

I'd like you to compare and contrast these photographs, and say how important you think the telephone is to these people.

Remember, *(Candidate B)*, you have only about a minute for this, so don't worry if I interrupt you. All right?

Candidate B: [*One minute.*]

Interlocutor: Thank you.

(Candidate A), do you use the telephone a lot?

Candidate A: [*Approximately twenty seconds.*]

Interlocutor: Thank you.

Part 3   (approximately 3 minutes)

Interlocutor: Now, I'd like you to talk about something together for about three minutes. I'm just going to listen.

Here is a picture of an island holiday resort and some ways of getting around.

Indicate the set of pictures 2E on pages C6–C7 of the Student's Book to the candidates.

First, talk to each other about the advantages and disadvantages of the different ways of getting around. Then decide which three would be best for seeing as much of the island as possible.

You have only about three minutes for this. So, once again, don't worry if I stop you, and please speak so that we can hear you. All right?

Candidates
A & B: [*Three minutes.*]

Interlocutor: Thank you.

Part 4   (4 minutes)

Interlocutor: *Select any of the following questions as appropriate.*

- Have you ever used any of these means of transport?
- Would you choose to go to a small island for a holiday?
- How active do you like to be on holiday?
- Do you think it's important for people to travel? Why (not)?
- What's the worst holiday you've ever had?
- Are there unusual holidays in your country?

Thank you. That is the end of the test.

Test 3

Note: In the examination, there will be both an assessor and an interlocutor in the room.

The visual material for **Test 3** appears on pages C9–C12 of the Student's Book.

Part 1   (3 minutes)

Interlocutor: Good morning/afternoon/evening. My name is .... and this is my colleague, ... He/she is just going to listen to us.

And your names are ... ?

Could I have your mark sheets, please?

Thank you.

First of all, we'd like to know something about you, so I'm going to ask you some questions about yourselves.

EITHER (non-UK-based candidates) OR   *(UK-based candidates)*

(Candidate A), do you live in .... ?   Where are you from, *(Candidate A)*?
(name of town where examination is being held)
And you, *(Candidate B)*?   And you, *(Candidate B)*?

- What do you like about living *(here / name of candidate's home town)*?
- And what about you, *(Candidate A/B)*?

(Select one or more questions from any of the following categories as appropriate.)

Home and family
- Is there anything you dislike about living in this area?
- Where do you think you'll be this time next year?
- Tell me something about your family.
- What would you like to change about your home?

Daily life and special occasions
- Tell me about your friends.
- Do you have any plans for next weekend?
- Do you normally celebrate special occasions with friends or family? (Why?)
- What did you do on your last birthday?
- What's the next special occasion you're going to celebrate?

Work/education
- What do you do in *(candidate's home town)*, do you work or study?

EITHER (if candidate is already working)
- What do you do?
- What do you like most about your job?
- What do you think you'll be doing in five years' time?

OR (if candidate is still studying)
- What subjects are you studying at the moment?
- What do you enjoy about *(one of the subjects named by the candidate)*?

- Are you looking forward to leaving school/college? Why (not)?
- What kind of job are you hoping to do in the future?

Health
- How much exercise do you do?
- How easy do you think it is to keep fit and healthy? Why?
- Do you think people are too interested in keeping fit today?

Interests
- What do you like to do in your free time?
- Do you have enough time to do all the things you enjoy?
- How often do you go to the cinema? *(If they go)* Have you seen any good films recently?
- How have your interests changed in the last few years?
- If you could choose to do something new, what would it be? Why?

Holidays
- Where did you go for your last holiday? Did you enjoy it?
- What kind of things do you like doing on holiday?
- How important is it to have good weather while you're on holiday?
- Are you planning to go anywhere special soon?

Part 2 (4 minutes)

Interlocutor:	Now, I'd like each of you to talk on your own for about a minute.
	I'm going to give each of you two different photographs and I'd like you to talk about them. *(Candidate A)*, here are your two photographs. They show different places in the evening.
	Indicate pictures 3A and 3B on page C9 of the Student's Book to (Candidate A).
	Please let *(Candidate B)* see them.
	(Candidate B), I'll give you your photographs in a minute.
	(Candidate A), I'd like you to compare and contrast these photographs, and say which place you'd prefer to spend an evening in.
	Remember, you have only about a minute for this, so don't worry if I interrupt you. All right?
Candidate A:	[*One minute.*]
Interlocutor:	Thank you.
	(Candidate B), do you enjoy evenings in the city?
Candidate B:	[*Approximately twenty seconds.*]
Interlocutor:	Thank you.
	Now, *(Candidate B)*, here are your two photographs. They show different special occasions. Please let *(Candidate A)* have a look at them.

Indicate pictures 3C and 3D on page C12 of the Student's Book to Candidate B.

I'd like you to compare and contrast these photographs, and say what you think the people will remember about these occasions.

Remember, *(Candidate B)*, you have only about a minute for this, so don't worry if I interrupt you. All right?

Candidate B:	[*One minute.*]
Interlocutor:	Thank you.

(Candidate A), do you enjoy special occasions?

Candidate A:	[*Approximately twenty seconds.*]
Interlocutor:	Thank you.

Part 3 (approximately 3 minutes)

Interlocutor: Now, I'd like you to talk about something together for about three minutes. I'm just going to listen.

Here are some pictures of people who are at the top of their professions.

Indicate the set of pictures 3E on pages C10–C11 of the Student's Book to the candidates.

First, talk to each other about how difficult it is to be successful in these professions. Then decide in which profession it is most difficult to get to the top.

You have only about three minutes for this. So, once again, don't worry if I stop you, and please speak so that we can hear you. All right?

Candidates A & B:	[*Three minutes.*]
Interlocutor:	Thank you.

Part 4 (approximately 4 minutes)

Interlocutor: *Select any of the following questions as appropriate.*

- What are the advantages of being famous?
- Which famous person do you most admire?
- How important is luck if you want to be successful?
- How important is it for people to have dreams and ambitions?
- Some people become famous when they are very young. What problems do you think this might cause?
- As well as being successful at work, what other things in life make people happy?

Thank you. That is the end of the test.

Test 4

Note: In the examination, there will be both an assessor and an interlocutor in the room.

The visual material for **Test 4** appears on pages C13–C16 of the Student's Book.

Part 1   (3 minutes)

Interlocutor: Good morning/afternoon/evening. My name is ………… and this is my colleague …………… . He/she is just going to listen to us.

And your names are … ?

Could I have your mark sheets, please?

Thank you.

First of all, we'd like to know something about you, so I'm going to ask you some questions about yourselves.

EITHER (non-UK-based candidates)   OR   (UK-based candidates)

(Candidate A), do you live in …… ?   Where are you from, *(Candidate A)*?
(name of town where examination is being held)
And you, *(Candidate B)*?   And you, *(Candidate B)*?

- What do you like about living *(here / name of candidate's home town)*?
- And what about you, *(Candidate A/B)*?

(Select one or more questions from any of the following categories as appropriate.)

Home and family
- Is there anything you dislike about living in this area?
- Where do you think you'll be this time next year?
- Tell me something about your family.
- What would you like to change about your home?

Daily life and special occasions
- Tell me about your friends.
- Do you have any plans for next weekend?
- Do you normally celebrate special occasions with friends or family? (Why?)
- What did you do on your last birthday?
- What's the next special occasion you're going to celebrate?

Work/education
- What do you do in *(candidate's home town)*, do you work or study?

EITHER (if candidate is already working)
- What do you do?
- What do you like most about your job?
- What do you think you'll be doing in five years' time?

OR (if candidate is still studying)
- What subjects are you studying at the moment?
- What do you enjoy about *(one of the subjects named by the candidate)*?

- Are you looking forward to leaving school/college? Why (not)?
- What kind of job are you hoping to do in the future?

Health
- How much exercise do you do?
- How easy do you think it is to keep fit and healthy? Why?
- Do you think people are too interested in keeping fit today?

Interests
- What do you like to do in your free time?
- Do you have enough time to do all the things you enjoy?
- How often do you go to the cinema? *(If they go)* Have you seen any good films recently?
- How have your interests changed in the last few years?
- If you could choose to do something new, what would it be? Why?

Holidays
- Where did you go for your last holiday? Did you enjoy it?
- What kind of things do you like doing on holiday?
- How important is it to have good weather while you're on holiday?
- Are you planning to go anywhere special soon?

Part 2   (4 minutes)

Interlocutor: Now, I'd like each of you to talk on your own for about a minute.

I'm going to give each of you two different photographs and I'd like you to talk about them. *(Candidate A)*, here are your two photographs. They show different public events.

Indicate pictures 4A and 4B on page C13 of the Student's Book to Candidate A.

Please let *(Candidate B)* see them.

(Candidate B), I'll give you your photographs in a minute.

(Candidate A), I'd like you to compare and contrast these photographs, and say which event you think would be more exciting to watch.

Remember, you have only about a minute for this, so don't worry if I interrupt you. All right?

Candidate A: [*One minute.*]

Interlocutor: Thank you.

(Candidate B), do you like watching public events?

Candidate B: [*Approximately twenty seconds.*]

Interlocutor: Thank you.

Now, *(Candidate B)*, here are your two photographs. They show two young people at home. Please let *(Candidate A)* have a look at them.

Indicate pictures 4C and 4D on page C16 of the Student's Book to Candidate B.

I'd like you to compare and contrast these photographs, and say what they show about the different interests of the young people.

Remember, *(Candidate B)*, you have only about a minute for this, so don't worry if I interrupt you. All right?

Candidate B:	[*One minute.*]
Interlocutor:	Thank you.
	(Candidate A), are you interested in football?
Candidate A:	[*Approximately twenty seconds.*]
Interlocutor:	Thank you.

Part 3   (approximately 3 minutes)

Interlocutor:	Now, I'd like you to talk about something together for about three minutes. I'm just going to listen.

Here are some pictures suggesting what friends are for.

Indicate the set of pictures 4E on pages C14–C15 of the Student's Book to the candidates.

First, talk to each other about the advantages of having friends. Then decide in which situations friends are most important.

You have only about three minutes for this. So, once again, don't worry if I stop you, and please speak so that we can hear you. All right?

Candidates A & B:	[*Three minutes.*]
Interlocutor:	Thank you.

Part 4   (approximately 4 minutes)

Interlocutor:	*Select any of the following questions as appropriate.*

- Are friends more important than family? Why (not)?
- What are the advantages of having friends older or younger than you?
- What sort of problems can having friends cause?
- What is the difference between a friend and a best friend?
- How do relationships change as people get older?
- How does your behaviour change when you're with people you don't know?

Thank you. That is the end of the test.

Test 1 Key

Paper 1   Reading (1 hour 15 minutes)

Part 1

1 F   2 D   3 B   4 H   5 G   6 A   7 E

Part 2

8 A   9 C   10 D   11 B   12 B   13 C   14 D

Part 3

15 C   16 G   17 E   18 H   19 B   20 A   21 F

Part 4

22 C   23 B   24 A   25/26 A/B (*in either order*)   27 B
28/29 C/D (*in either order*)   30/31 B/C (*in either order*)
32/33 A/C (*in either order*)   34/35 C/E (*in either order*)

Paper 2   Writing (1 hour 30 minutes)

Task-specific mark schemes

Part 1

Question 1
Content
Major points: The letter must include the following points.
1) the pen and pencil are not very attractive
2) the name is misspelt
3) the pen and pencil do not match
4) the gift arrived too late
5) the writer must ask for their money back

Organisation and cohesion
Letter format, with early reference to why the person is writing. Suitable paragraphing. Clear organisation of points. Suitable opening and closing formulae.

Appropriacy of register and format
Formal letter.

Range
Language of complaint, explanation and request.

Target reader
Would understand the nature and detail of the complaint and would have enough information to consider the request for a refund.

Part 2

Question 2

Content

Composition could agree or disagree with the proposition, or discuss both sides of the argument.

Range

Language of opinion, explanation and description. Vocabulary relevant to clothes.

Organisation and cohesion

Clear development of viewpoint with appropriate paragraphing and linking of ideas.

Appropriacy of register and format

Neutral composition.

Target reader

Would be able to understand the writer's viewpoint.

Question 3

Content

Article should suggest one of the four ideas given for a club and state why the writer is choosing that idea. There should also be one other idea (either from the list or the writer's own idea), with the reason for suggesting that idea.

Range

Language of suggestion and explanation.

Organisation and cohesion

Clear development of ideas, with appropriate linking and paragraphing.

Appropriacy of register and format

Register could range from the informal to the formal, but must be consistent throughout.

Target reader

Would know which clubs the writer would like to see started after school and why.

Question 4

Content

Report should give factual information about things for visitors to see and do in the writer's area in one day (acceptable to mention just one thing).

Range

Language appropriate to giving information and making suggestions.

Organisation and cohesion

Report should be clearly organised. Sub-headings would be an advantage, if not, suitable paragraphing. There should be an introduction and a conclusion.

Appropriacy of register and format
Formal report layout is not essential. Register could range from the neutral to the formal, but must be consistent throughout.

Target reader
Would know what to do in the writer's area in one day.

Question 5(a)

Content
Writer can agree or disagree with the proposition that the characters are believable and should explain their opinion with reference to the book or short story read.

Range
Language of opinion and explanation.

Organisation and cohesion
Clear development of viewpoint with appropriate paragraphing and linking of ideas.

Appropriacy of register and format
Neutral composition.

Target reader
Would be able to understand the writer's point of view.

Question 5(b)

Content
Letter should give information about the book or short story/stories and state whether the writer would recommend it or not to their friend to read. The writer should also give reasons for their recommendation or lack of recommendation.

Range
Language of narration, description and explanation.

Organisation and cohesion
Letter format, with early reference to why the person is writing. Clear organisation of points. Suitable opening and closing formulae. Appropriate paragraphing.

Appropriacy of register and format
Informal letter.

Target reader
Would be informed about the book or short story/stories and would know whether it would be a good choice to read and why.

Paper 3   Use of English (1 hour 15 minutes)

Part 1

1 A	2 D	3 B	4 C	5 B	6 C	7 A	8 C
9 D	10 B	11 B	12 C	13 C	14 B	15 B	

Part 2

16 where   17 when/while   18 with   19 and   20 so   21 as
22 would   23 something   24 for   25 without/avoiding
26 having/facing/experiencing   27 up   28 a   29 since/because/as
30 had

Part 3

31 in **order** | to be
32 is | no **point**
33 **until** | we had finished/done
34 was **better** | than Tim
35 if | she **does** not do OR unless | she **does**
36 if/whether he realised | **what** time
37 **put** an advertisement | for
38 **finished** his speech | before thanking OR **finished** (his speech) | by thanking
39 has been / is | a **month** since
40 **following** their | appearance

Part 4

41 been   42 which   43 ✓   44 hardly   45 ✓   46 had
47 have   48 ✓   49 last   50 extra   51 out   52 those
53 ✓   54 myself   55 because

Part 5

56 variety   57 director   58 inhabitants   59 choice/choices
60 growth   61 unemployment   62 agreement   63 loss
64 unable   65 decision

Paper 4   Listening (40 minutes approximately)

Part 1

1 A   2 A   3 C   4 B   5 C   6 B   7 C   8 A

Part 2

9 graves   10 twelfth century   11 their/the owners
12 make(-)up   13 ten thousand pounds
14 original clothes   15 soft bodies
16 maker(')s name(s)   17 (little) adults   18 plastic

Part 3

19 E   20 F   21 D   22 B   23 C

Part 4

24 J   25 TT   26 J   27 J   28 TT   29 A   30 J

Transcript

First Certificate Listening Test. Test One.
Hello. I'm going to give you the instructions for this test. I'll introduce each part of the test and give you time to look at the questions. At the start of each piece you'll hear this sound:

tone

You'll hear each piece twice.

Remember, while you're listening, write your answers on the question paper. You'll have time at the end of the test to copy your answers onto the separate answer sheet.

There will now be a pause. Please ask any questions now, because you must not speak during the test.

[pause]

Now open your question paper and look at Part One.

[pause]

PART 1

You'll hear people talking in eight different situations. For questions 1 to 8, choose the best answer, A, B or C.

Question 1

One.
You hear part of a radio play.
Where is the scene taking place?
A   in the street
B   in a bank
C   in a police station

[pause]

tone

Policeman:	So what happened, madam?
Woman:	Well, I saw this old man, he was kind of holding this briefcase under his arm, like this. He'd just left the bank and I was still queuing up to collect my pension, but I was near that door. Now, this young man came running past him and grabbed him by the arm.
Policeman:	And they both fell down?
Woman:	Yeah, and the young man ran away and the poor old man sat on the pavement, still clutching his briefcase, and we managed to help him up. Now, can I go back in to collect my money?
Policeman:	Would you mind coming with us, madam? We need a few more details.

[pause]

tone

[The recording is repeated.]

[pause]

Question 2	*Two.*
	You overhear the beginning of a lecture.
	What subject are the students taking?
	A medicine
	B sport
	C music

[pause]

tone

Woman: It's important that you really listen to what people are telling you. For example, I had a trumpet player who came to see me with back pain and breathing difficulties. He couldn't take his final exams because of the muscular tension in his jaw, but when I quizzed him about it, it turned out that the actual problem was in his teeth – far away from where the pain actually was. The same applies to sports people who often have injuries as a result of their job …

[pause]

tone

[The recording is repeated.]

[pause]

Question 3	*Three.*
	You overhear a conversation in a college.
	Who is the young man?
	A a new student
	B a student in the middle of a course
	C a former student

[pause]

tone

Man: It all looks so different. Where's the canteen?

Woman: It's in the basement. You get there by going down the main staircase from the entrance hall.

Man: Right. I'll get there in the end. Everything seems to have moved around.

Woman: Yes, there was a re-building programme last year, which wasn't much fun for those of us trying to study. The main building was altered a lot. And they're building a new sports centre. It should be open for the new students in September.

Man: Well, I'm envious. Everything looks a lot better.

[pause]

tone

[The recording is repeated.]

[pause]

Question 4   Four.
You hear a woman on the radio talking about a cookbook.
What does she regret?
A   not looking after it
B   not having kept it
C   not using it properly

[pause]

tone

Woman: I used to watch granny cooking, and right from when I was five years old, I was allowed to season the soups, test the potatoes and so on. One year for my birthday, she bought me a cookbook. It was just like granny talking; all the recipes were simple, economical and linked with little stories, useful advice and amusing sketches. I treasured it, but gradually it fell to bits from overuse, my tastes changed and, finally, I threw it out. Now, of course, I wish I'd hung on to it despite its sad state and despite the fact that all the advice would be out of date.

[pause]

tone

[The recording is repeated.]

[pause]

Question 5   Five.
You hear someone talking about the day he met someone famous.
How did he feel after meeting Chris Turner?
A   unimpressed with the footballer
B   angry with his friend
C   disappointed with himself

[pause]

tone

Man: I went to a party with a friend and she knows that I'm a big fan of Chris Turner, the footballer. I just think he's a genius and, anyway he was going to be there. Now, I knew that I would be really shy, which is stupid because he's exactly the same age as me and, you know, he's just a regular bloke, I'm sure. But when my friend introduced us and he shook my hand, my mouth just went, you know, really dry and I didn't know what to say, honestly, which was awful. I felt so bad about it afterwards, my friend just couldn't understand it.

[pause]

tone

[The recording is repeated.]

[pause]

Question 6   Six.
                 You hear a woman talking on the phone.
                 Why has she called?
                 A   *to request a meeting*
                 B   *to offer assistance*
                 C   *to apologise for her absence*

                 [pause]

                 tone

Woman: Hi, can I just talk to you about our plans for the Summer Conference? I think I
                 said that I was going to be away for the opening meeting and couldn't give you a
                 hand, but it seems I got my diary muddled up and I will actually be around, so
                 what would you like me to do?

                 [pause]

                 tone

                 [The recording is repeated.]

                 [pause]

Question 7   Seven.
                 You overhear an extract from a radio play.
                 What is the young woman's relationship with the man?
                 A   *She's a pupil of his.*
                 B   *She's a relative of his.*
                 C   *She's a patient of his.*

                 [pause]

                 tone

Man: So, Sophie, tell me all about it.
Woman: I'm sorry, but I've just been feeling terrible for the last week or so and last night I
                 just couldn't do my homework, I felt so bad. I was aching all over. So my Dad
                 said I had better make an appointment and come and see you. Perhaps you can
                 tell me what's wrong.

                 [pause]

                 tone

                 [The recording is repeated.]

                 [pause]

Question 8   Eight.
                 You hear someone telling a story about a strange thing that happened in the
                 mountains.
                 What point does the story prove?
                 A   *how strange things can be explained simply*
                 B   *how easy it is to imagine things*
                 C   *how you can be tricked by the silence*

[pause]

tone

Man: My wife Margaret and I were sitting behind a rock on the top of a mountain in the Highlands one day, nobody else around, perfectly silent, and Margaret said, 'I just heard a telephone bell ringing.' 'Oh,' I said, 'Margaret, there are no telephone kiosks up here.' But in the silence of the hills, you can imagine anything. I said, 'I often imagine things. I've heard babies crying in this silence. I've thought I heard a symphony orchestra,' and Margaret said, 'I'm sure I heard a telephone ringing.' She got up and went round the back of the rock and there was a cow with a bell around its neck.

[pause]

tone

[The recording is repeated.]

[pause]

That's the end of Part One.

Now turn to Part Two.

[pause]

PART 2   *You'll hear part of a talk about dolls. For questions 9 to 18 complete the sentences.*
      You now have forty-five seconds in which to look at Part Two.

[Pause the recording here for 45 seconds.]

tone

Man: Dolls have always fascinated me, and that's why, five years ago, I was delighted to be offered the job of running a doll museum.
     Dolls have existed for thousands of years, and the earliest dolls we know about were found in graves in ancient Egypt. I only wish we could get one or two for our museum, but we haven't unfortunately, got anything as old as that in the museum. All the same, we have got examples from Europe from the twelfth century, but my favourite early dolls are actually from the seventeenth century. They interest me not just because they are early, or fairly early, but also because of the clothes they're wearing. They have their original clothes, and from them we know what the owners wore, since dolls in those days were always dressed like their owners. They were made of the only material readily available for things like this at the time: solid wood, and they were painted in great detail. In fact, on the best examples, like the ones in the museum, the detail includes the seventeenth century make-up.
     Dolls like these were very expensive then, and only the very rich could afford them. These days, they're popular with collectors and if you want one today, you have to pay anything up to £10,000 for a doll in perfect condition from this time! By the way, what makes them so valuable is that, as far as a collector is concerned, a doll is only worth collecting if it is in perfect condition, and that means having the original clothes.

Doll collecting has become very fashionable since the museum opened, with people interested in dolls from every period, including later dolls. There's great interest in nineteenth century examples, when dolls were no longer made of wood, but began to have soft bodies and real hair. They were very delicate and few have survived, meaning such a doll would be worth about £2000, perhaps a bit more. Later, in the nineteenth century, you could often take off the doll's hair. If you can, you can often see the maker's name underneath, and of course the right one increases a doll's value.

There was a really big change in dolls at the beginning of the twentieth century. In the museum we have one of the earliest examples, from about 1909, of a doll that's a model of a baby. Previously all dolls, the earlier ones, were little adults. That's just one of the changes that have occurred in the last hundred years. Another, again, is to do with what dolls are made of. Although dolls with soft bodies continued, after about 1930, plastic began to be used. In fact, dolls from the 1930s and 40s are now very popular with collectors, some of them selling for very, very high prices.

[pause]

Now you'll hear Part Two again.

tone

[The recording is repeated.]

[pause]

That's the end of Part Two.

Now turn to Part Three.

[pause]

PART 3

You'll hear five different people talking about why they decided to become nurses. For questions 19 to 23, choose which of the reasons A to F each speaker is giving. Use the letters only once. There's one extra letter which you do not need to use.

You now have thirty seconds in which to look at Part Three.

[Pause the recording here for 30 seconds.]

tone

Speaker 1

[pause]

Well I have to say, I never really thought about a career until I got to my last year at school. Lots of people here say that they knew exactly what they wanted to do right from a very young age, but I never really had any burning ambitions. In the end I just sort of drifted into it because that's what our lot have always done. If I'd chosen something else – like going into business, say – I would have been the first for four generations to have gone outside the medical field. I don't think that that would have mattered but it means there are lots of things we can talk about at home.

[pause]

Speaker 2

[pause]

Most of my friends went into teaching actually – I think they felt it was more 'academic' and of course the pay is quite a bit better. But I've never really been bothered about things like that – I think the enjoyment of the job comes first and I certainly get a lot of good feelings doing this work. We have some difficult cases sometimes but there's still a lot of laughter here and the patients can be amazing – especially the kids. I'd recommend it to anyone who likes helping people.

[pause]

Speaker 3

[pause]

I think I'm lucky really because I didn't try very hard at school – I guess you'd call me lazy! And then it ended and I thought 'Wow, I'd better think about a job,' and I got really worried and emotional about it because, well, I suddenly realised that I didn't want to go from job to job, you know. I wanted a career and regular money and an opportunity to climb up the ladder if possible. So, one day I saw a TV programme about nursing and it looked like it had the kind of benefits that I wanted – so here I am.

[pause]

Speaker 4

[pause]

At first I thought I'd made the wrong choice … you know, I was never really sure that it was the thing for me and I used to go back to my flat at night and think – well maybe I should have listened to my parents after all. They thought I'd get too upset and that I should have stuck with something office-based like the rest of my family but it was my best subject at school – well Biology was – and all the staff there thought medicine would be a good choice, so … Anyway, one day I woke up and felt fine about it and it's been great ever since.

[pause]

Speaker 5

[pause]

I remember we all had to go to this Careers Advisor in our last year at school and I think she got really confused when she saw me because I just had no idea. I liked the sound of a lot of jobs and I couldn't make up my mind. When the time came to tell our teachers what we were going to apply for, I thought – well what *does* matter to me is being separate from my friends and so I went round to see one of them – the most important I suppose, and anyway she had chosen nursing, so that was it really – a difficult decision made easy, although I must say, I've never regretted it.

[pause]

Now you'll hear Part Three again.

tone

[The recording is repeated.]

[pause]

That's the end of Part Three.

Now turn to Part Four.

[pause]

PART 4   *You'll hear part of a radio programme in which a book critic gives information about three new books on the subject of travelling in the United States of America. For questions 24 to 30, decide which book each statement refers to. Write A for A TO Z, J for JUST GO or TT for TRAVEL TREAT.*

You now have forty-five seconds in which to look at Part Four.

[Pause the recording here for 45 seconds.]

tone

Critic: Well, this week we have three new travel guides about the USA, *A to Z to the USA* by Peter Tongue, *Just Go* by Carol Brand and *Travel Treat* by John Barnes. Travel guides should give us not just all the practical details, but also background information, and *Just Go* manages to pack in more of the latest developments in public life, civic affairs and government than the usual guide. For some reason, *Travel Treat* and *A to Z* tend to ignore this. Though it must be said that *Travel Treat* does give you a good insight into the American way of life.

With travel guides I tend to feel that the writer's experience is crucial. Now, these three writers are young, but when you read *A to Z*, what strikes you is that the author is a sophisticated world traveller who has clocked amazing mileage throughout thirty countries and four continents.

Nevertheless, there's a feeling that this time he has not put in as much work prior to writing. And you have the same impression with *Just Go*. *Travel Treat*, on the other hand, seems to be based on an incredible amount of serious work, although the author is not nearly as widely travelled.

Some travel guide books manage to take travellers away from the tourist trail, and *Just Go* is outstanding in this respect, with extensive coverage of areas which other guides don't think worth mentioning. To be fair, *A to Z* also tries to encourage you to depart from the beaten track, but it doesn't succeed quite as well.

Travel Treat can at times be a bit on the dull side, while *Just Go* tries to be funny without really succeeding. *A to Z*, however, is one of those books where, although I'm sure it wasn't the author's intention that we should laugh, you just can't help seeing the funny side of some of the misfortunes of this enthusiastic traveller!

All the guides give good advice on health. In *Just Go* and *A to Z*, you are told what to do about drugs, the heat … all the important details. In addition to that, *Travel Treat* also tells you about the kind of medical insurance you need to take out before you go.

Well, next, I think all three travel guides make a real effort to provide tips about where to go for entertainment. *A to Z* is particularly good for people travelling on a tight budget because it tells you how to avoid all the tourist traps … and still see the best shows in town. *Just Go* tends to concentrate more on the upmarket end of the scale, and so does *Travel Treat*, although both of them have some very good advice.

And finally, I think from this point of view, *Just Go* gives the reader the whole range of options, from staying with families to luxury hotels for those who can afford it. *A to Z* and *Travel Treat* are not as comprehensive, but they both have a very good section on activity holidays, staying on farms or ranches.

[pause]

Now you'll hear Part Four again.

tone

[The recording is repeated.]

[pause]

That's the end of Part Four.

There'll now be a pause of five minutes for you to copy your answers onto the separate answer sheet.

[Pause the recording here for five minutes. Remind your students when they have one minute left.]

That's the end of the test. Please stop now. Your supervisor will now collect all the question papers and answer sheets.

Goodbye.

Test 2 Key

Paper 1   Reading (1 hour 15 minutes)

Part 1

1 G   2 E   3 B   4 H   5 F   6 A   7 D

Part 2

8 B   9 B   10 D   11 C   12 A   13 A   14 D   15 C

Part 3

16 F   17 A   18 C   19 G   20 D   21 E

Part 4

22 D   23 A   24 D   25/26 C/E (*in either order*)   27 B   28 E
29/30 A/B (*in either order*)   31 C   32/33 B/D (*in either order*)   34 C
35 D

Paper 2   Writing (1 hour 30 minutes)

Task-specific mark schemes

Part 1

Question 1

Content
Major points: Letter must include all the points in the notes.
1) commenting on the choice of hotel
2) suggesting food for the party
3) explaining why a watch is not a good idea for a present and/or suggesting something else
4) apologising for not being able to help the day before
5) suggesting something else for the party

Organisation and cohesion
Letter format, with early reference to why the person is writing. Clear organisation of points. Suitable opening and closing formulae.

Appropriacy of register and format
Informal letter.

Range
Language appropriate for making suggestions, giving reasons and apologising.

Target reader
Would be informed about the writer's ideas for the party.

Part 2

Question 2

Content
Composition could agree or disagree with the proposition, or discuss both sides of the argument.

Range
Language of opinion and explanation. Vocabulary relevant to transport.

Organisation and cohesion
Clear development of viewpoint with appropriate paragraphing and linking of ideas.

Appropriacy of register and format
Neutral composition.

Target reader
Would be able to understand the writer's point of view.

Question 3

Content
Letter should explain why the writer is a suitable person for the job.

Range
Language of explanation, giving information and personal description.

Organisation and cohesion
Clear presentation and organisation in the letter. Suitable opening and closing formulae.

Appropriacy of register and format
Formal or semi-formal letter.

Target reader
Would have enough information to assess writer's suitability for the job.

Question 4

Content
Story should end with the prompt sentence.

Range
Past tenses. Vocabulary appropriate to the chosen topic for the story.

Organisation and cohesion
Could be minimally paragraphed. Should reach a definite ending, even if that ending is somewhat open-ended, as in many modern short stories.

Appropriacy of register and format
Consistent neutral or informal narrative.

Target reader
Would be able to follow the storyline.

Question 5(a)

Content
Composition should discuss the importance of the title of the book or short story and why the writer chose that title.

Range
Language of narration, description and explanation.

Organisation and cohesion
Clear development of ideas, with appropriate linking and paragraphing.

Appropriacy of register and format
Neutral composition.

Target reader
Would be informed about the importance of the title of the book or short story and why the author chose that title.

Question 5(b)

Content
Report on book or short story, either recommending it or not recommending it for members of the English book club.

Range
Language of giving information, description, narration and perhaps recommendation.

Organisation and cohesion
Report should be clearly organised. Sub-headings would be an advantage. There should be an introduction and a conclusion.

Appropriacy of register and format
Register could range from formal to informal, but must be consistent throughout. Formal report layout is not essential.

Target reader
Would be informed about the book or short story and whether the book is suitable to include on the list or not.

Paper 3   **Use of English** (1 hour 15 minutes)

Part 1

1 C	2 B	3 D	4 C	5 B	6 D	7 B	8 A
9 B	10 D	11 A	12 A	13 D	14 C	15 C	

Part 2

16 because   17 more   18 of   19 are   20 too
21 be/sound   22 when/while/as   23 which   24 had/needed
25 what   26 again   27 would   28 if/provided   29 first
30 by

Part 3

31 would **like** | to know
32 **let** us | park (our car)
33 if | I had **seen**
34 **there** is | a hole in
35 was **called** | off
36 pays (any/much) **attention** | to
37 if she | would **lend** him OR to | **lend** him
38 **might** have | forgotten
39 **efficient** at | checking
40 (single) child | has (great) **fun**

Part 4

41 for   42 ✓   43 much   44 if   45 ✓   46 own   47 to
48 that   49 eat   50 the   51 ✓   52 ✓   53 at   54 it   55 ✓

Part 5

56 frequently   57 impressive   58 comfortable   59 flight(s)
60 communications   61 increasingly   62 improvement(s)
63 noisy   64 Crowded/Overcrowded   65 unfortunately

Paper 4   Listening (40 minutes approximately)

Part 1

1 A   2 A   3 C   4 B   5 A   6 B   7 C   8 C

Part 2

9 March   10 design   11 publicity
12 (in) (the) (two) meeting(s) rooms   13 £35   14 teachers
15 adults   16 acting   17 Ewington CORRECT SPELLING ONLY
18 (the) Education Manager

Part 3

19 F   20 B   21 A   22 E   23 C

Part 4

24 B   25 C   26 A   27 A   28 C   29 B   30 C

Transcript

First Certificate Listening Test. Test Two.

Hello. I'm going to give you the instructions for this test. I'll introduce each part of the test and give you time to look at the questions. At the start of each piece you'll hear this sound:

tone

You'll hear each piece twice.

Remember, while you're listening, write your answers on the question paper. You'll have time at the end of the test to copy your answers onto the separate answer sheet.

There will now be a pause. Please ask any questions now, because you must not speak during the test.

[pause]

PART 1

Now open your question paper and look at Part One.

[pause]

You'll hear people talking in eight different situations. For questions 1 to 8, choose the best answer, A, B or C.

Question 1

One.
You overhear two people talking in a restaurant.
Where has the woman just come from?
A   *a supermarket*
B   *a hospital*
C   *a football match*

[pause]

tone

Woman:	I felt so sorry for her, she just couldn't cope. She had the baby under one arm and a list in the other. And he was screaming, all red in the face. She must have only just come out of hospital, he was so tiny.
Man:	So you offered to help.
Woman:	Well, I wanted to get through the check-out and pay for my things quickly, otherwise I knew I'd be late getting here, but …
Man:	Well, I've only been here half an hour.
Woman:	Oh, I'm sorry, there was such a queue. And then I forgot, it's the big football game today and the roads were just packed …

[pause]

tone

[The recording is repeated.]

[pause]

Question 2   *Two.*
                You hear a man talking about a mobile phone he has bought.
                What most attracted him to this phone?
                A   its size
                B   its reliability
                C   its price

                [pause]

                tone

    Man: I've never wanted to walk around with an enormous mobile, you know, fixed to
                my belt or whatever, because that's socially embarrassing, isn't it? So I was
                really taken with the Edmundsen GP 876 model which you can just slip in your
                inside pocket and no one's the wiser, if you know what I mean. And it says in the
                blurb 'satisfaction guaranteed – should your mobile develop a fault in the first
                year, we will replace it the next day'. Well, to be honest, it wasn't exactly what
                you call cheap, so I'm rather hoping that I don't need to find out just how good
                that particular promise is.

                [pause]

                tone

                [The recording is repeated.]

                [pause]

Question 3   *Three.*
                You hear a man talking on the phone about buying a house.
                What is the purpose of his call?
                A   to apologise
                B   to complain
                C   to obtain information

                [pause]

                tone

    Man: Hello, it's Mr Brown here. I got your message. Yes, I was really sorry to hear the
                house I wanted had just been sold … Yes … I missed the chance to buy the
                house of my dreams. Yes, I know it wasn't your fault. I should have contacted
                you earlier. … Yes … That's why I'm now eager to hear of any houses that come
                on the market. As you know, what I want is a house which combines a kitchen
                and breakfast room with lots of space for living, eating and cooking. … Yes, I'm
                tired of small places where you can hardly move.

                [pause]

                tone

                [The recording is repeated.]

                [pause]

Question 4

Four.
You hear a teenage girl talking about her hobby.
What is she talking about?
A   a computer game
B   a musical instrument
C   a piece of sports equipment

[pause]

tone

Girl: I got it as a present from my father when I was fourteen. My family thought it would be a phase, that I'd go off the idea. Mum doesn't believe there'll be any money in it, but Dad is quite interested because, apart from football, it's the only thing I can talk to him about at the moment. If you're not going to make the effort to practise on it, no way is anyone going to be interested in you. I think one of the reasons you see so few girls playing in bands is that they tend not to be willing to do all that work.

[pause]

tone

[The recording is repeated.]

[pause]

Question 5

Five.
On the news, you hear a story about a cat.
Where was the cat found?
A   in a train carriage
B   on the railway lines
C   on a station platform

[pause]

tone

Newsreader: A cat with a mind of its own joined the 11.55 train from King's Lynn yesterday. A passenger spotted the cat, thought to have boarded at Littleport, and handed it to a member of the platform staff once the train got to Ely station. The friendly cat was put in a box and returned to Littleport. Eventually, its owner, Jack Prince, from Littleport, was reunited with his cat. It is thought that the cat must have crossed the lines at Littleport and waited on the platform, together with a dozen passengers who didn't notice it at all.

[pause]

tone

[The recording is repeated.]

[pause]

Question 6

Six.
You hear a woman talking about how she gets ideas for her work.

Who is the woman?
A   a novelist
B   an artist
C   a film-maker

[pause]

tone

Woman: I work with my husband, Bob, and every time we have a holiday somewhere, we seem to come up with an idea. And touring round the USA last year, he'd written the words for this children's ghost story. But I had no idea how to … to get the atmosphere in the pictures, which is my role in the partnership. And then we went to Las Vegas and all that amazing architecture, lit up at night under the desert sky, was er … was dreamlike. I mean, despite all the films, nothing prepares you for what it actually feels like to be there. I just sat down and started sketching out ideas on the spot.

[pause]

tone

[The recording is repeated.]

[pause]

Question 7   *Seven.*
You hear two people talking.
How does the woman feel?
A   surprised
B   satisfied
C   relieved

[pause]

tone

Woman: There they are! At last. I've been looking for them everywhere.
Man: What? Your keys? You're always losing them.
Woman: I know, and I really thought I'd lost them for good this time. Thank goodness!
Man: Why don't you make sure you put them down in the same place, then you'd have the satisfaction of finding them whenever you wanted them.
Woman: Maybe. That's not a bad idea. I'll think about it.

[pause]

tone

[The recording is repeated.]

[pause]

Question 8   *Eight.*
You turn on the radio and hear a man speaking.
What are you listening to?

A   *a history programme*
B   *a science-fiction story*
C   *an advertisement*

[pause]

tone

Man: Discover the amazing secrets of the planet Earth in three major recently launched exhibitions: 'From the Beginning', 'Earth's Treasury' and 'Earth Today and Tomorrow' which form the finest series of exhibitions of their kind in the world. Together they tell Earth's dramatic story, starting with the birth of the universe, exploring the forces that shape it and the riches within it, concluding with a glimpse into the future and what it might hold for our planet.

[pause]

tone

[The recording is repeated.]

[pause]

That's the end of Part One.

Now turn to Part Two.

[pause]

PART 2   *You will hear a radio interview with a woman who is organising a training weekend for people interested in the theatre. For questions 9 to 18, complete the notes.*

You now have forty-five seconds in which to look at Part Two.

[Pause the recording here for 45 seconds.]

tone

Interviewer: If you've ever dreamt of directing a play or designing a stage set, well the opportunity has arisen for you and who knows where it could lead. My next guest, Claire Ewington, from the local theatre, is here to tell us more about a practical weekend training event to start your dreams rolling, you might say. Good afternoon, Claire.
Claire: Good afternoon.
Interviewer: So, when is the training weekend and what does it involve?
Claire: It's the first weekend in March and there are two days of activities with a choice of activities on each day. The Saturday is either 'Design', which means a whole day working with a professional designer, or 'Directing' with a professional director and they'll be looking at the day to day workings of each of the professions with a chance to get involved. The same on Sunday, a full day of activities again, 'Make-up' or 'Press and publicity' are the choices.
Interviewer: And where will the course be taking place?
Claire: Well, each group will spend some time working on the stage, but actually we spend most of the time in two meeting rooms at the theatre. We can take up to 25 in either group on either day, so that's a total of 50 people each day.

Interviewer: Okay. And how long does it last, each session?

Claire: Each session is ten till five, with lunch breaks and coffee breaks included.

Interviewer: How much does a weekend training event cost?

Claire: For the participants it's £20 per day including lunch, and if you book for the two days, it's £35 including lunch on both days.

Interviewer: Do you reckon that the training would be enough to set a person up in a new career within the theatre or whatever?

Claire: I think it would certainly help you decide if you'd thought about doing it, whether or not it's for you, because they are professionals who are leading the course, but they are also trained teachers – so they know how to get the message across. So, whether you've had experience or not, it might just set your mind thinking and suggest some new avenues maybe.

Interviewer: Are you looking for any particular age group?

Claire: Well, what we are generally saying is that this course is directed at adults especially, but any youngsters who've been working in this sort of activity are very welcome to come along.

Interviewer: Right. Have you had successful events like this before?

Claire: We ran a training day last year, when the focus was on acting and it was very, very successful and because of that, we came up with the idea of running another course.

Interviewer: So, for people listening to this who'd like to be involved in this year's training weekend, how do they apply?

Claire: If you're interested, whether you've got any experience or not, do ring me. My name is Claire Ewington …

Interviewer: I'll just make a note of this because if I write the listeners will have time to do so as well.

Claire: … and that's spelt E-W-I-N-G-T-O-N and your best bet is to phone me directly at the theatre for more information or to book your place. And it's a city number, so that's 01773 578926.

Interviewer: And you're the Education Manager at the theatre, aren't you?

Claire: That's right and, of course, we have many other educational projects throughout the year.

Interviewer: So, anyone interested in those could also call you.

Claire: Indeed.

Interviewer: Thank you very much, Claire, and all the best for the training weekend.

Claire: Thank you.

[pause]

Now you'll hear Part Two again.

tone

[The recording is repeated.]

[pause]

That's the end of Part Two.

Now turn to Part Three.

[pause]

PART 3   *You will hear five different students who are studying away from home. They are talking about their accommodation. For questions 19 to 23, choose from the list A to F what each speaker says about their accommodation. Use the letters only once. There is one extra letter which you do not need to use.*

You now have thirty seconds in which to look at Part Three.

[Pause the recording here for 30 seconds.]

tone

Speaker 1

[pause]

I'd requested college accommodation, so when I was offered it I was really pleased. I didn't fancy having to look after myself … too many other things to do … lessons and homework and going out with friends. I knew what the rules were – in by ten, no noise after nine – and I didn't mind them at first, but they've started to annoy me more and more – and now I can't wait to get out and be able to do my own thing. I don't think I'll be recommending this place to anyone else!

[pause]

Speaker 2

[pause]

It's exciting leaving home and becoming independent. I've been staying with some relatives for the past year. I'd stayed with them before so when I knew I was coming here to study they said, why don't you come and live with us – great. And they've been fine – let me do whatever I want and haven't stuck to rigid meal times and all that sort of thing. So I've been able to meet plenty of people and get to know the area and the course and so on. I feel a part of it all now, but I'm always ready to try something different.

[pause]

Speaker 3

[pause]

I was pretty calm about coming here, but I couldn't decide whether to stay with a family or get my own flat. I'd talked to other people, you know, friends who've studied away from home before and they all recommended that I should get a flat because you have so much more freedom, so I did that. I'd only been here two weeks and I went out one day and left the front door unlocked. When I got back, I found that my camera had been stolen. I suppose I was lucky it was just that. I'm a bit more careful now.

[pause]

Speaker 4

[pause]

My friend Benny and I started the course at the same time. There was never any doubt that we'd share a place. It was the obvious choice for us to make and I think it's definitely the best option. Of course, you have to think about what you're going to eat, have some kind of system for cleaning, a few ground rules. We get annoyed with each other at times. Benny smokes and I had to ask him to go outside, which he does now. It hasn't all been straightforward but overall I prefer the independence this place gives me.

[pause]

Speaker 5

[pause]

My sister came here before me and studied at the same college. She told my parents that it would be much better if I stayed with her and then she could look after me, help me settle down here, that kind of thing. So, that's what happened – nobody asked me what I wanted to do. Well, the truth is we don't get on badly but I never seem to see the other students that I study with, which is a big disadvantage. I think it's better to force yourself to find your own way in a new environment.

[pause]

Now you'll hear Part Three again.

tone

[The recording is repeated.]

[pause]

That's the end of Part Three.

Now turn to Part Four.

[pause]

PART 4   *You will hear part of a radio interview in which Tina White, a magazine editor, talks about her life and work. For questions 24 to 30, choose the best answer A, B or C.*

You now have one minute in which to look at Part Four.

[Pause the recording here for one minute.]

tone

Interviewer:	Tina White, some people describe you as the best magazine editor in the world, and you are only in your thirties. Can you tell us how you started your amazing career?
Tina:	Well, when I was twenty, still at college, I was asked to write a weekly column for a local paper. The paper had wanted me to write about famous people, you know, their wonderful lifestyles, the sort of thing people like to read about. Instead, what I did was to concentrate on people who the general public didn't know, but who had something original to say.

Interviewer: And you got away with it! Now at that early stage, your family was important. How far did they influence your career choice?

Tina: My father was a film producer, and my childhood was spent around international actors and directors, so with such influences, I should have become an actress – something my father would have loved. But no, I chose to be a journalist in spite of the wishes of my family. I think the biggest influence was my school, not so much the people but the materials it gave me access to … the hours and hours spent in the library.

Interviewer: From being a journalist, you then went on to become an editor. I understand the first magazine you edited, *Female Focus*, wasn't much of a success?

Tina: Well, I was the editor for a year, and then I resigned, mainly because of disagreements with the owners. They were reluctant to change things, because they had faith it would eventually make a profit. But when you think of it, the magazine had been losing millions of pounds a year before I became its editor. When I left, it was still losing money but nothing like as much as previously. Also, when I took over, it was selling around 650,000 copies. That soon increased to 800,000, so it was certainly an improvement.

Interviewer: And now you are editing *Woman's World*, and you've made it the best selling women's magazine ever. How do you make people want to read it?

Tina: For some of my competitors, the most important point is what you put on the cover of your magazine. But they forget faithful readers look beyond that. The real challenge is, how do you encourage a reader to read a serious piece? How are we going to make it an article that people want to read? You have to get their attention. And nothing does that better than a very lively, even shocking, opening line.

Interviewer: It is said that you work very hard because you don't trust your employees.

Tina: That *was* the case five years ago, when I was appointed. It almost drove me mad. I knew I had the right idea, for example, but I wasn't able to get it done because I didn't have the brilliant writers I have now, or the right staff to read all the material when it came in. I had to read everything about six times, and that was awful! It took me four years to put together the team I wanted, and it would be very unfair to say I don't trust them.

Interviewer: Do you sometimes worry that you might lose your fame and wealth?

Tina: Yes, when you work as an editor, you are praised today and criticised tomorrow. Of course it would be difficult to live without all the … well … material comforts I'm used to, but a smaller income is something I think I could cope with. It wouldn't be the end of the world. Much more serious would be if the people I work with no longer admired my work, and most of all I want it to stay that way.

Interviewer: And what about the future?

Tina: Well, people often think I have planned my career very carefully, but in fact lots of things have happened by chance. Lots of opportunities have come my way, and I was once asked to edit a book series. As a youngster, one of my dreams was to be a writer, to write a novel that would become a best-seller and then an award-winning film. Well, it may seem silly, but I still hope that will happen one day.

Interviewer: Tina, thank you very much for joining us today.

[pause]

Now you'll hear Part Four again.

tone

[The recording is repeated.]

[pause]

That's the end of Part Four.
There'll now be a pause of five minutes for you to copy your answers onto the separate answer sheet.

[pause]

[Teacher, pause the recording here for five minutes. Remind your students when they have one minute left.]

[pause]

That's the end of the test. Please stop now. Your supervisor will now collect all the question papers and answer sheets.

Goodbye.

Test 3 Key

Paper 1   Reading (1 hour 15 minutes)

Part 1

1 C   2 H   3 F   4 A   5 G   6 E   7 B

Part 2

8 C   9 A   10 A   11 B   12 D   13 C   14 A   15 B

Part 3

16 F   17 H   18 E   19 A   20 C   21 G   22 B

Part 4

23 C   24 D   25 A   26 B   27/28 C/D (*in either order*)
29 C   30 B   31 E   32 F   33 E   34/35 F/D (*in either order*)

Paper 2   Writing (1 hour 30 minutes)

Task-specific mark schemes

Part 1

Question 1

Content
Major points: Letter must include all the points in the notes.
1) recommend the earlier trip, as it is less crowded
2) explain why a guided tour is essential
3) suggest taking a picnic
4) suggest trying water sport(s)
5) give information about group booking

Organisation and cohesion
Letter format, with early reference to why the person is writing. Clear organisation of points. Suitable opening and closing formulae.

Appropriacy of register and format
Informal letter.

Range
Language appropriate for recommending, giving reasons, making a suggestion and giving information.

Target reader
Would have enough information to decide about the trip.

Part 2

Question 2

Content
Report should give suggestions about how often the club should meet, what type of activities it should organise and how the club could be advertised.

Range
Language of making suggestions and vocabulary appropriate to organising an English language club.

Organisation and cohesion
Report should be clearly organised. Sub-headings would be an advantage. There should be an introduction and a conclusion.

Appropriacy of register and format
Register could range from the neutral to the formal, but must be consistent throughout. Formal report layout is not essential.

Target reader
Would be informed about the writer's suggestions for the organisation of the club.

Question 3

Content
Story should continue from the prompt sentence.

Range
Past tenses. Vocabulary appropriate to chosen topic for story.

Organisation and cohesion
Could be minimally paragraphed. Story should reach a definite ending, even if that ending is somewhat open-ended, as in many modern short stories.

Appropriacy of register and format
Consistent neutral or informal narrative.

Target reader
Would be able to follow the storyline.

Question 4

Content
Article should describe the difference it would make in the writer's life to have to live without television for a week.

Range
Language of description and comparison.

Organisation and cohesion
Clear development of description with appropriate linking and paragraphing.

Appropriacy of register and format
Register could range from informal to neutral, but must be consistent throughout.

Target reader
Would be informed about the difference the lack of television would make to the writer.

Question 5(a)

Content
Writer should say whether anything in the book or short story disappointed him/her.

Range
Language of description and narration.

Organisation and cohesion
Clear organisation of composition with appropriate paragraphing.

Appropriacy of register and format
Neutral composition.

Target reader
Would be informed about whether the candidate was disappointed or not with reference to the book or short story read.

Question 5(b)

Content
Clear reference to characters from the book or short story and the importance of the relationships between them.

Range
Language of description, narration and explanation of views.

Organisation and cohesion
Clear development of description and narration leading up to explaining the candidate's viewpoint, with appropriate linking and paragraphing.

Appropriacy of register and format
Neutral composition.

Target reader
Would be informed about the importance of the relationships between characters.

Paper 3 Use of English (1 hour 15 minutes)

Part 1

1 C	2 B	3 B	4 C	5 D	6 B	7 C	8 C	9 A
10 D	11 A	12 C	13 D	14 C	15 B			

Part 2

16 did/tried   17 with/over   18 such   19 to   20 those
21 only/just   22 could/would   23 in   24 as   25 were
26 it   27 nothing   28 but/although   29 which   30 for

Part 3

31 be produced | **by** this company
32 to talk | to him **again**
33 **my** holiday | I had

34 **ought** to | have locked
35 any **chance** | of Pete
36 from Paul | **nobody** has
37 got | **used** to
38 **felt** like | doing
39 being **unable** | to sing
40 as **soon** as | we arrive

Part 4

41 place 42 being 43 in 44 have 45 by 46 ✓
47 which 48 had 49 either 50 there 51 it 52 of
53 having 54 too 55 ✓

Part 5

56 attractive 57 tourists 58 achievement 59 employee
60 originality 61 communication(s) 62 unclear 63 traditional
64 success 65 appearance

Paper 4   Listening (40 minutes approximately)

Part 1
1 C 2 B 3 A 4 B 5 B 6 A 7 C 8 B

Part 2
9 south of France 10 1970 11 famous people 12 (young) children
13 (about) 50% 14 under (the) water 15 breathe (out) 16 (try to) float
17 (feeling) confident 18 3 hours/lessons

Part 3
19 C 20 B 21 D 22 F 23 E

Part 4
24 F 25 T 26 F 27 F 28 F 29 T 30 T

Transcript   *First Certificate Listening Test. Test Three.*
Hello. I'm going to give you the instructions for this test. I'll introduce each part of the test and give you time to look at the questions. At the start of each piece you'll hear this sound:

tone

You'll hear each piece twice.

Remember, while you're listening, write your answers on the question paper. You'll have time at the end of the test to copy your answers onto the separate answer sheet.

There will now be a pause. Please ask any questions now, because you must not speak during the test.

[pause]

PART 1   *Now open your question paper and look at Part One.*

[pause]

You'll hear people talking in eight different situations. For questions 1 to 8, choose the best answer, A, B or C.

Question 1   *One.*
You overhear a man talking about an experience he had at an airport.
What did he lose?
A   his passport
B   his wallet
C   a piece of luggage

[pause]

tone

Man: The airport staff looked everwhere for it. It was terrible. I thought the plane was going to go without me. At first I thought someone must have taken it. Although my money wasn't inside, I'd bought some nice presents for the family. Then I remembered that I'd been to the washroom and I must have put it down in there. Luckily, I had my documents and boarding card in my jacket pocket and, to cut a long story short, I had to get on the plane without it. The airport staff sent it on to me three days later.

[pause]

tone

[The recording is repeated.]

[pause]

Question 2   *Two.*
You hear an advertisement on the radio.
What is special about the Fretlight guitar?
A   It plays recorded music.
B   It teaches you how to play.
C   It plugs into a computer.

[pause]

tone

Man: The *Fretlight* is a fully functional guitar that comes in acoustic and electric models. Built into its body is an on-board computer and 132 lights that show you where to put your fingers. Simply flip a switch and choose the chord or note that you would like to play, and the finger positions for making the appropriate notes will be promptly displayed on the neck of the guitar. Beginners can get a real feel for the fingerboard, while the more experienced players will be able to discover lots of new musical possibilities …

[pause]

tone

[The recording is repeated.]

[pause]

Question 3	*Three.* *You hear part of a radio programme.* *What is the presenter talking about?* *A food safety* *B meal times* *C healthy recipes*

[pause]

tone

Presenter: Whether you have just one large meal a day, or a number of small meals, there are some basic steps to keep you in good health. Ideally, eat food as soon as it is cooked or prepared. If you are preparing food for later use, keep cold foods in the fridge and hot foods hot until they are ready to be eaten. Piping hot, that's how cooked food should be, especially when it's reheated. And remember, prepared foods left at room temperature will not keep long, however fresh the ingredients you have used.

[pause]

tone

[The recording is repeated.]

[pause]

Question 4	*Four.* *You hear two people discussing a type of pollution.* *What do the speakers agree about?* *A the best way to solve the problem* *B how they feel about this type of pollution* *C how they reacted to the solution they saw*

[pause]

tone

Woman: Do you know what they were doing in town the other day? I had to rush away because it set my teeth on edge, but they were chipping the chewing gum off the paths with sharp tools.

Man: You know, I only realised recently that all those black spots on the ground are actually old chewing gum.

Woman: I mean, it's disgusting, isn't it?

Man: Deeply.

Woman:	And what a nasty job!
Man:	Well, I was actually there when the city once tested out a machine for this and, I had to laugh, it needed such a powerful suck to get it off, it lifted the stones themselves.

[pause]

tone

[The recording is repeated.]

[pause]

Question 5

Five.
You hear a conversation between a shop assistant and a customer about a compact disc.
What was the cause of the problem?
A The customer gave the wrong number.
B A mistake was made on the order form.
C The disc was incorrectly labelled.

[pause]

tone

Shop asst:	And you ordered it two weeks ago? Well, I can't find anything in the order book … Oh, yes, here it is. Well, it seems we chased it up after you phoned and they said they couldn't find the order, so we gave them the details again. It hasn't turned up though. Oh, perhaps … here's a note on the order form. They then told us there's nothing under the number you gave us, I'm afraid.
Customer:	Well, I noted it down very carefully. Look.
Shop asst:	Uh-huh. Oh, I see. Two figures are the wrong way round on our form, that's why they couldn't find the disc.

[pause]

tone

[The recording is repeated.]

[pause]

Question 6

Six.
You overhear a conversation at a football game.
What does the speaker say about his team?
A They're better than usual.
B They're as good as he expected.
C They tend to be unlucky.

[pause]

tone

Man 1:	Not many here today, are there?

Man 2: I guess it isn't as popular as it used to be. A few years ago it was so crowded here, you were lucky if you could see over all the heads. This is the first time I've been this season. I was expecting to see them lose – as ever – but I can't wait for the second half if they carry on playing like this.

[pause]

tone

[The recording is repeated.]

[pause]

Question 7 | *Seven.*
You overhear a schoolgirl talking to her friend.
What does she think about her new teacher?
A   He is clever.
B   He is funny.
C   He is interesting.

[pause]

tone

Girl: It's funny, I've had loads of maths teachers and they all seemed to be the same – really clever with figures but useless at dealing with children. That's why I used to play about in lessons and do anything for a laugh. But Mr Jones is something else. He's quite serious and he makes us work really hard and gives us loads of problems to solve, but what I like is he relates everything to real life.

[pause]

tone

[The recording is repeated.]

[pause]

Question 8 | *Eight.*
In a hotel you overhear a conversation.
Who is the woman?
A   a tour guide
B   a tourist
C   a hotel receptionist

[pause]

tone

Man: Oh, by the way, what's this all-island trip like then?
Woman: It lasts all day and you get picked up from the hotel at about 7.30 and they take you around the island to look at the sights.
Man: Do you think it's worth going on then?
Woman: I'd say so. You see all the sights and have lunch in a restaurant by the sea. The price includes everything, you know, like the museum and everything. The whole family enjoyed it when we went.

[pause]

tone

[The recording is repeated.]

[pause]

That's the end of Part One.

Now turn to Part Two.

[pause]

PART 2   *You will hear part of a radio interview with a swimming instructor. For questions 9 to 18, complete the sentences.*

You now have forty-five seconds in which to look at Part Two.

[Pause the recording here for 45 seconds.]

tone

Interviewer:	And now for our sports section, and I have with me today Paul Collison who is a swimming instructor with a rather unusual approach. Thanks for taking the time during your holiday to come and talk to us, Paul.
Paul:	It's very kind of you to invite me.
Interviewer:	Paul – you're *the* swimming instructor at the Palace Hotel in the south of France. How long have you been there?
Paul:	Oh, well I started working there in 1970 when I was 18 years old.
Interviewer:	And you've never moved?
Paul:	Nope – I get to meet a lot of famous people there and … I guess I enjoy that.
Interviewer:	And of course a lot of them go there because they want *you* to teach them to swim!
Paul:	That's true, but I teach plenty of other people too – and not all my students are beginners.
Interviewer:	But we're not talking about young children, are we?
Paul:	Not usually – there isn't the same challenge teaching children. They have an almost natural ability to swim. Adults are afraid, and helping them overcome that is hard but much more fun somehow.
Interviewer:	But don't a lot of people just give up trying to learn once they reach a certain age?
Paul:	Not at all. I get hundreds of calls from people looking for 'sympathetic' instructors. I would estimate that about 50% of the adult population can't swim – but they're still keen to learn.
Interviewer:	So it's just fear that holds them back?
Paul:	Basically, yes. I come across it all the time and it isn't just beginners. I have students who can swim a bit, but don't make any progress because – like all of them – they hate going *under* water.
Interviewer:	Mmm … So what's the secret, Paul?
Paul:	Well, you've got to relax in the water and that means that you *must* control your breathing.
Interviewer:	And I understand you have a special technique to help people do that.
Paul:	Yes, before my students even go into the pool I teach them how to breathe and to do that I give everyone a salad bowl.
Interviewer:	A salad bowl? Right …

Paul:	Everyone in the group gets one of these … each full of water. First, I get them to breathe … slowly through the nose and mouth … just normal controlled breathing.
Interviewer:	To calm them.
Paul:	Uhuh … and then – they all have to put their faces in the bowl and breathe out under water.
Interviewer:	How does it go?
Paul:	Well, they're all terrified at first. So we repeat the exercise many times and in the end they become quite competitive about who can keep their face down the longest!
Interviewer:	And that means they've started to forget about their fear.
Paul:	Exactly. When I'm sure they're more confident about breathing, I move the group into the pool and I tell them that they are going to begin by trying to float with their faces in the water. Once I'm sure they're OK, I start them off and I teach different swimming strokes to different pupils depending on which one I think they'll find easiest. The swimming technique itself is far less important than feeling confident in the water.
Interviewer:	Great. So how many lessons would I need to learn to swim?
Paul:	Well, all my lessons are an hour long and generally it just takes three to overcome the fear and get people swimming. A few never make it but I'd say 90% end up swimmers.
Interviewer:	So there's hope for us all yet … and now on to …

[pause]

Now you'll hear Part Two again.

tone

[The recording is repeated.]

[pause]

That's the end of Part Two.

Now turn to Part Three.

[pause]

PART 3   *You'll hear part of a radio programme called 'Morning Market'. Five listeners have telephoned the programme because they have something to sell. For questions 19 to 23, choose which of the statements A to F matches the reason each of the people gives for selling their possession. Use the letters only once. There's one extra letter which you do not need to use.*

You now have thirty seconds in which to look at Part Three.

[Pause the recording here for 30 seconds.]

tone

Speaker 1

[pause]

I've got a brand-new rowing machine. I won it actually, about two months ago, and it's still in its box. It's got an electric timer on it which tells you how much rowing you've done and all that. So anyone who's into exercise can do lots of rowing and keep fit and healthy. It folds up really small, so, you know, it won't take up too much space in, like, a bedroom or anything. I mean, I'll never use it because I was after the holiday which was won by whoever came first in the competition. So I'm looking for around forty-five pounds and my number is …

[pause]

Speaker 2

[pause]

I've got a kidney-shaped bath, colour soft cream, for sale. It's still in its original packing case because I ordered the wrong colour, you know, it didn't go with the rest of the bathroom suite I'd got. So, I contacted, you know, the suppliers who said they'll send me a replacement, at a price, of course! But I've now got to get rid of this one. It cost originally a hundred and seventy-five pounds and I'm letting it go for fifty if anyone's interested. OK? My number's …

[pause]

Speaker 3

[pause]

I've got a real bargain. It's a Lieberstein electric organ and it's got two keyboards and a rhythm section. It's in good condition, plays quite well, and it's not difficult to use or anything. But, what with us having a baby on the way, it's got to make way for more essential items, as we've only got a tiny flat at the moment. So, as I say, if anyone wants it, they can make me an offer. The only problem is anyone interested would have to come and collect it. The number to ring is …

[pause]

Speaker 4

[pause]

Hallo. I've got a ladies' cycle for sale. I've got back trouble and I've been advised not to ride it, so rather than be tempted, I'll get rid of it. I hate the idea, because we're not well-served with public transport out here and I used it quite a lot, but as I daren't ride it any more, I think it would be a mistake to hang on to it, you know, in case I had second thoughts. So, it's a Raleigh Chopper, pink, and I'd like thirty-five pounds for it, please. I can be contacted on …

[pause]

Speaker 5

[pause]

I've got two frying pans, you know, the sort for cooking stir-fry in, and a seven-piece tool set to go with them. All boxed and everything. Anyway, they've hardly been used because at one time I was intending to do a lot of this type of cooking because I've only got a small kitchenette, like, no oven. But I've been given a microwave instead now, so much easier to use. So, that's ten pounds for both pans and the tools and my number is …

[pause]

Now you'll hear Part Three again.

tone

[The recording is repeated.]

[pause]

That's the end of Part Three.

Now turn to Part Four.

[pause]

PART 4   *You'll hear a radio interview with Peter Manson about the job he does for a record company. For questions 24 to 30, decide which of the statements are TRUE and which are FALSE. Write T for TRUE or F for FALSE.*

You now have forty-five seconds in which to look at Part Four.

[Pause the recording here for 45 seconds.]

tone

Interviewer: So, Peter, as far as I understand it, with record companies in Britain fiercely competing to find good new bands, your job is to look for talented young musicians?

Peter Manson: That's right. In the 1980s, record companies stopped actively looking for new talent because they were reissuing old hits on compact disc, but now that is no longer profitable.

Interviewer: So now they are employing people like you?

Peter Manson: Yes, when we find a good artist or band, we sign them up, that is we sign a contract with them. There's a flood of small bands and other new artists. I recently signed up an 18-year-old schoolboy who had produced two excellent recordings from his bedroom! My job is not an easy one because surprisingly most young artists are really quiet people, not at all out-going and they try to avoid publicity.

Interviewer: How do you find your new bands?

Peter Manson: Well, it's a bit of a lottery. One will turn up when you're not even looking for it. That's what makes life interesting for me. I'll give you an example. In the summer of 1993, I happened to be in a record shop in Oxford, and I met a guy that played bass for a local band called 'Loops'. A few days later I went to see them play in a tent on Oxford Park, as part of an extremely wet music festival. The band proved to be superb.

Interviewer: So you signed them up for your company?

Peter Manson: Well, they had begun to be followed around by other 'talent spotters' like myself. It took me three months from when I first saw them, before I could persuade them to sign a contract. They liked me, but the main reason was I had seen them first. That sort of thing makes it all worthwhile.

Interviewer: So do things ever get nasty?

Peter Manson:	Well, I'm not perfect, but some people in the music business will do dishonest things. One of my competitors once went as far as sending expensive presents to a band he and I wanted to sign up.
Interviewer:	Do you rely on contacts for information?
Peter Manson:	Oh, certainly. Lots of contracts will result from information I get from contacts. But you must make sure they are good sources. Once I found myself in a threatening situation, when two big, strong men brought a tape into my office and demanded I listen to it. For six months after that I received frightening threats.
Interviewer:	So your life is not as glamorous as it seems …
Peter Manson:	Well, in my profession, we spend a lot of time at musical venues, but in fact we can't just relax and enjoy ourselves. You find yourself going to more and more shows, hoping to spot someone a bit special. You often don't even see the whole show as you can quickly spot those with talent and those without.
Interviewer:	It must be exhausting!
Peter Manson:	Yes, we live in fear of not attending the obscure show that might have led to the big, important contract, missing the little band who might just turn out to be the next week's heroes. Sometimes you miss things simply by not being early enough. And of course all the time we must also look after the bands we already have contracts with.
Interviewer:	Well, you seem to be doing extremely well, anyway.
Peter Manson:	Oh, yes! My greatest moment was only a couple of months ago. This band, having only played together a couple of times, drove to this venue and demanded to be allowed to play a song. I was in the audience, they started to play, and after hearing just a few notes on the guitar, shouted that I'd just discovered the future of rock 'n' roll and jumped on the stage to sign them! Fortunately it turned out later that they could sing as well!
Interviewer:	The story must bring tears to your rivals' eyes. Well, we certainly wish you the best of luck with this new band! Peter Manson, thank you very much for talking to us.

[pause]

Now you'll hear Part Four again.

tone

[The recording is repeated.]

[pause]

That's the end of Part Four.
There'll now be a pause of five minutes for you to copy your answers onto the separate answer sheet.

[Teacher, pause the recording here for five minutes.
Remind your students when they have one minute left.]

That's the end of the test. Please stop now. Your supervisor will now collect all the question papers and answer sheets. Goodbye.

Test 4 Key

Paper 1 Reading (1 hour 15 minutes)

Part 1

1 C 2 A 3 G 4 B 5 F 6 H 7 E

Part 2

8 B 9 C 10 A 11 D 12 A 13 B 14 C 15 C

Part 3

16 B 17 C 18 E 19 H 20 D 21 F 22 A

Part 4

23 C 24 D 25 B 26 A 27 E 28 A 29 C
30 A 31 D 32 C 33 B 34 E 35 D

Paper 2 Writing (1 hour 30 minutes)

Task-specific mark schemes

Part 1

Question 1

Content
Major points: The letter must:
1) be positive about the good programme arranged by Mr Robertson
2) point out at least one thing especially appreciated
3) explain that all the students would like to go to the London Fashion and Leisure Show
4) give at least one reason why they want to go
5) suggest how the programme could be changed.
N.B. Coverage of the first point may not explicitly include 'thanks'. The 'thanks' may be implicit.

Organisation and cohesion
Letter format, with early reference to why the person is writing. Clear organisation of points with suitable paragraphing. Suitable opening and closing formulae.

Appropriacy of register and format
Formal letter.

Range
Language appropriate for explaining, making a request and making a suggestion.

Target reader
Would have enough information to act on and respond to the writer's letter.

Part 2

Question 2

Content
Composition could agree or disagree with the proposition, or discuss both sides of the argument.

Range
Language of opinion and explanation. Vocabulary relevant to the way the topic is explored.

Organisation and cohesion
Clear development of viewpoint with appropriate paragraphing and linking of ideas.

Appropriacy of register and format
Neutral composition.

Target reader
Would be able to understand the writer's viewpoint.

Question 3

Content
Article should state ways in which people's homes in the future will be different and/or ways in which they might be the same. (Acceptable to say or imply that nothing will be the same.)

Range
Language of description. Possibly explanation. Vocabulary relating to homes / the future.

Organisation and cohesion
Clear development of ideas, with appropriate linking and paragraphing.

Appropriacy of register and format
Register could range from the informal to the formal, but must be consistent throughout.

Target reader
Would be clearly informed.

Question 4

Content
Story should continue from the prompt sentence in the first person.

Range
Past tenses. Vocabulary appropriate to the chosen topic for the story.

Organisation and cohesion
Could be minimally paragraphed. Should reach a definite ending.

Appropriacy of register and format
Consistently neutral or informal narrative.

Target reader
Would be able to follow the storyline.

Question 5(a)

Content
Writer can agree or disagree with the statement, and explain why with reference to the book or story read.

Range
Language of opinion and explanation.

Organisation and cohesion
Clear development of viewpoint with appropriate paragraphing and linking of ideas.

Appropriacy of register and format
Neutral composition.

Target reader
Would be able to understand the writer's point of view.

Question 5(b)

Content
Writer should inform their pen friend whether the book or short story read would be a suitable present for the pen friend's cousin's fifteenth birthday.

Range
Language of opinion, explanation and possibly recommendation.

Organisation and cohesion
Clear development of viewpoint with appropriate paragraphing and linking of ideas.

Appropriacy of register and format
Informal letter.

Target reader
Would be informed as to whether to give the book or short story as a present to the fifteen-year-old.

Paper 3   Use of English (1 hour 15 minutes)

Part 1

1 D	2 C	3 D	4 B	5 D	6 C	7 B	8 C
9 C	10 D	11 A	12 B	13 C	14 D	15 D	

Part 2

16 take   17 not   18 been   19 need/have   20 of/with/in
21 each   22 far   23 While/As/When   24 are/get   25 on
26 the/these   27 get/climb   28 in   29 which   30 first/times

Part 3

31 **took** my car | didn't
32 never seen | such a **strange**
33 were **driven** | into town by
34 **insisted** on | paying
35 didn't **succeed** | in persuading
36 you **mind** | not using
37 not seen Mark **since** | last
38 made a **good** | impression on
39 **wishes** (that) he had | told
40 had **trouble** | (in) following

Part 4

41 who   42 ✓   43 ✓   44 for   45 all   46 ✓
47 just   48 ✓   49 out   50 they   51 much   52 any
53 by   54 been   55 ✓

Part 5

56 extraordinary   57 freezing/frozen   58 assistance   59 equipment
60 loneliness   61 hopeful   62 friendships   63 heat
64 poisonous   65 reasonable

Paper 4   Listening (40 minutes approximately)

Part 1

1 A   2 A   3 B   4 A   5 C   6 A   7 C   8 C

Part 2

9 circle (around them)   10 (a) brain(s)   11 stress
12 feelings   13 read   14 reward   15 52 teeth   16 two days
17 sound wave(s)/sound(s) / high-pitched noises   18 (fishing) nets

Part 3

19 E   20 F   21 C   22 D   23 B

Part 4

24 A   25 C   26 B   27 A   28 A   29 C   30 B

Transcript
First Certificate Listening Test. Test Four.
Hello. I'm going to give you the instructions for this test.
I'll introduce each part of the test and give you time to
look at the questions. At the start of each piece you'll hear
this sound:

tone

You'll hear each piece twice.

Remember, while you're listening, write your answers on
the question paper. You'll have time at the end of the test
to copy your answers onto the separate answer sheet.

There will now be a pause. Please ask any questions now,
because you must not speak during the test.

[pause]

Now open your question paper and look at Part One.

[pause]

PART 1
You'll hear people talking in eight different situations. For
questions 1 to 8, choose the best answer, A, B or C.

Question 1
One.
You overhear some people talking at a party in a hotel.
Where did the people first meet each other?
A   at school
B   at work
C   at a wedding

[pause]

tone

Man: Is Mark Hobson here?

Woman: He's got a crisis at work and couldn't come. But Julie's here
somewhere. Did you know he married Julie? You know, the girl
who could never spell anything!
Man: Oh, right.
Woman: It's their wedding anniversary today, actually. She says she'd
rather be here with her childhood friends than waiting at home
for Mark to finish work!
Man: Has he changed much?
Woman: Well, he looks much the same as he did all those years ago.

[pause]

tone

[The recording is repeated.]

[pause]

81

Question 2	*Two.*
	You overhear a conversation in a restaurant.
	Why haven't they seen each other lately?
	A *He has been too busy.*
	B *He has been ill.*
	C *He has been away.*

[pause]

tone

Man:	Hello, Jean!
Woman:	Mike Carstairs! My favourite customer. You haven't been in for ages.
Man:	No, I haven't, that's right.
Woman:	How are you?
Man:	I'm fine. I heard you weren't well.
Woman:	Well, I was away for a couple of weeks. But I'm fine now. Ah! You were going to the States, weren't you?
Man:	That fell through.
Woman:	Oh, did it?
Man:	What I've been doing is reorganising the whole department non-stop since I saw you. Just haven't had a moment to myself. This is the first time I've been in here since Christmas.
Woman:	Well, it's good to see you. Are you ready to order?

[pause]

tone

[The recording is repeated.]

[pause]

Question 3	*Three.*
	You overhear someone talking about a concert.
	How did she feel at the time?
	A *angry*
	B *frightened*
	C *disappointed*

[pause]

tone

Girl:	It was really awful and I'd been so looking forward to it. Don't get me wrong – the music was brilliant and the show itself was really well done, but I'm sure they let too many people in – it was ever so crowded. I was right at the front and everyone was pushing me against the stage. I couldn't breathe and I was so scared I thought I was going to faint.

[pause]

tone

[The recording is repeated.]

[pause]

Question 4　　Four.
　　　　　　　You hear a writer of children's stories talking about books and compact
　　　　　　　discs.
　　　　　　　What advantage does he think books have over compact discs?
　　　　　　　A　*They may last for a longer time.*
　　　　　　　B　*They are easier to look after.*
　　　　　　　C　*They contain better quality material.*

　　　　　　　[pause]

　　　　　　　tone

　　　Man:　　I was brought up with a respect for books, you know, always having clean hands,
　　　　　　　not bending the pages down, etc. and I certainly try to make sure mine are as
　　　　　　　well-made as possible. I like to pick them up by the wrong bit and throw them
　　　　　　　around and so on, you know, to make sure they are strong. I think it's the
　　　　　　　permanence of books that sets them apart from the other media, don't you? Of
　　　　　　　course, what's more important is that you have good literature and good images
　　　　　　　and, I suppose, whether that's actually on a compact disc or in a book doesn't
　　　　　　　matter.

　　　　　　　[pause]

　　　　　　　tone

　　　　　　　[The recording is repeated.]

　　　　　　　[pause]

Question 5　　Five.
　　　　　　　You hear a husband and wife talking about their summer holidays.
　　　　　　　What problem do they have?
　　　　　　　A　*They really hate flying anywhere.*
　　　　　　　B　*They can never think of anywhere to go.*
　　　　　　　C　*They never agree about what to do.*

　　　　　　　[pause]

　　　　　　　tone

　Husband:　You see right from the time we first met it was obvious that Natalie and I wanted
　　　　　　　a particular kind of holiday – the trouble was, it wasn't the same! I like going off
　　　　　　　and doing my own thing. You know, history and museums – that's what interests
　　　　　　　me.
　　　Wife:　Well, I love markets and looking for bargains – so we end up sort of hating each
　　　　　　　other for two weeks or so, instead of having a really nice time together. The odd
　　　　　　　thing is that we see eye to eye all the rest of the time. It's just when we step on
　　　　　　　that plane – then the trouble starts!

　　　　　　　[pause]

　　　　　　　tone

　　　　　　　[The recording is repeated.]

　　　　　　　[pause]

Question 6 | Six.
You hear a researcher being asked about her work.
What is she doing when she speaks?
A   denying an accusation
B   disproving a theory
C   accepting a criticism

[pause]

tone

Interviewer: Now it's a bit suspicious that this research about glasses has been paid for by a contact lens company, isn't it? Is it genuine or are you having us on?

Researcher: Not at all. We asked about a thousand people, most of whom wore glasses, some of whom didn't, and really asked them what they thought of glasses. Their responses were interesting, but didn't come from us; it's what they told us answering open-ended questions. And most of them said, while they thought that glasses could be, you know, pretty trendy and that some of them looked quite cool, that they didn't much like them.

[pause]

tone

[The recording is repeated.]

[pause]

Question 7 | Seven.
You overhear a woman talking to a friend on a train.
What does the woman think of the course she has attended?
A   It has made her feel more confident.
B   It has made her feel less confident.
C   It hasn't made much difference to how she feels.

[pause]

tone

Woman: Well, the whole point was to build confidence and I'm sure most feel it succeeded, even if only partly. I must say I found it all very enjoyable, although I can't say I've benefited greatly. There was plenty of opportunity to get to know other people in the business, though, if you wanted to – you know the sort of thing, trips to restaurants and the theatre in the evenings.

[pause]

tone

[The recording is repeated.]

[pause]

Question 8   *Eight.*
              You overhear a woman speaking on the radio.
              What is she doing?
              A   *complaining about something*
              B   *apologising for something*
              C   *explaining something*

              [pause]

              tone

Man: So, shall we move on to the next subject?
Woman: I'm sorry, but I do think it's necessary to go through this again for the benefit of
              your listeners. Look, this is a crucial point and I don't think it can be stressed
              enough. As I was saying, the first thing that anyone with a complaint about their
              pension should do is put it in writing.

              [pause]

              tone

              [The recording is repeated.]

              [pause]

              That's the end of Part One.

              Now turn to Part Two.

              [pause]

PART 2   *You'll hear a radio report about dolphins. For questions 9 to 18, complete*
              the sentences.

              You now have forty-five seconds in which to look at Part Two.

              [Pause the recording here for 45 seconds.]

              tone

Newsreader: And for our last news item today, a special report from Diane Hassan on an
              animal that is rapidly becoming known as 'man's best friend', the dolphin.
Diane: Last week, a 28-year-old diver who went swimming in the Red Sea with a group
              of dolphins, learnt the hard way just how caring these creatures can be. When
              the diver was suddenly attacked by a shark, they saved him by forming a circle
              around him and frightening the shark away.
                 It's not the first time such a rescue has happened and it's been known for
              some time that dolphins will do for humans what they do for their own kind. They
              are, in fact, the only animals in the world whose brains match ours in terms of
              size, and their intelligence and ability to feel emotion continue to fascinate
              scientists and doctors alike. For some time now, their healing powers have been
              well known. A swim with a group of dolphins, for example, is a recognised
              'medical' activity for everyday problems such as stress. But some dolphins are
              playing a far more serious medical role for us than that. Amanda Morton, who
              suffered from a life-threatening illness, argued that being with dolphins *saved her*
              life because they were able to read her feelings. 'They knew how I was feeling,'

85

she was quoted as saying. And it's the idea that they actually 'care', that they are gentle, happy creatures that want to befriend us, which has led to projects with children as well. In one such project, dolphins are being used to help children who are slow learners learn to read. The dolphins do things like carrying small boards on their noses. These boards show words or pictures which the children are asked to identify. When the children get it right, they spend more time swimming with the dolphins and touching them and they see this as a reward. So what is it that makes contact with dolphins so powerful? They certainly have an engaging smile … in each jaw they have up to 52 teeth, but rather than frightening us to death, it's one of the warmest greetings in the world! They're also fantastic swimmers to watch … the spotted dolphin has been observed reaching 20 miles an hour and keeping this up for two days at a time. And they _know_ they're good at it so they show off in front of humans by diving in and out of the water and showing us just how much fun they're having. They're great communicators too. They make all kinds of fascinating high-pitched noises. They catch fish, for example, by sending out sound waves which tell them everything they need to know – where it is, what it is and how big it is.

The only creatures that concern dolphins, in fact, are sharks and _man_. We don't necessarily harm them on purpose, but we trap them in fishing nets and we pollute the water they swim in. Pollution, in fact, is one of the dolphin's greatest problems. So with all the good they do for us, isn't it time we started caring about them?

[pause]

Now you'll hear Part Two again.

tone

[The recording is repeated.]

[pause]

That's the end of Part Two.

Now turn to Part Three.

[pause]

PART 3   _You'll hear five different people talking about the head teacher or principal of their former secondary school. For questions 19 to 23, choose from the list A to F what each speaker is saying. Use the letters only once. There's one extra letter which you do not need to use._

You now have thirty seconds in which to look at Part Three.

[Pause the recording here for 30 seconds.]

tone

Speaker 1

[pause]

It's strange looking back because at the time you don't always appreciate people and certainly I think that's true of your teachers and particularly a head teacher. I mean she was always encouraging us not to drop litter and to think about things like preserving the countryside and so on, and she'd say 'Don't you want your children to live in a better world?' But when you're fifteen, you can't imagine having a family – all you care about is getting your homework done and going out with your friends!

[pause]

Speaker 2

[pause]

I don't know if it's the same in all countries, but where I live your head teacher usually teaches classes too and we had our head for athletics. In one way it was exciting 'cos she was very good at it herself, like she could out-run any of the boys in our class, but whatever we were doing she was always pushing us to do it faster than anyone else or jump higher than our friends regardless of the talent or ability we had – and with some it was pointless.

[pause]

Speaker 3

[pause]

I think if it hadn't been for our head teacher, I'd be doing something quite different now. She used to assess our Art exams and although there were people in my class who were really talented artists … you know they could paint anything from real life and it looked brilliant … she always preferred the more unusual stuff – she said it showed we had ideas of our own, and she really liked that, so, I did well. I mean now I make a living putting designs on greeting cards.

[pause]

Speaker 4

[pause]

I always felt that our head teacher was under-valued and that she might have done better in a different environment … her own staff held her up a bit. They all seemed … oh, I don't know … maybe they just didn't like the idea of change … but I remember she wanted to introduce a new teaching method for French classes and the department head just dismissed the idea … and so many ideas she had which were never taken up are being used in schools today. I sometimes wonder how she feels.

[pause]

Speaker 5

[pause]

I've got some friends who say they left school and they suddenly felt lost. They'd spent a long time 'getting an education' but didn't know what to do once they'd got it. I think we were lucky because our head teacher built up a good network of contacts with local people and so they didn't mind giving us an insight into what it might be like, say, working in a hospital or office. I know it wasn't a new idea or anything but I think she gave us a good sense of direction which I've valued all my life.

[pause]

Now you'll hear Part Three again.

tone

[The recording is repeated.]

[pause]

That's the end of Part Three.

Now turn to Part Four.

[pause]

PART 4

You will hear an interview with a tour leader who works for an adventure company in Africa. For questions 24 to 30, choose the best answer A, B or C.

You now have one minute in which to look at Part Four.

[Pause the recording here for one minute.]

Announcer: And now for the holiday programme with Mandy Rice.

Mandy: Today I'm talking to Don Nicholson, a tour leader who spends 10 months of the year looking after groups of up to 18 tourists in southern Africa. They travel together in the back of a truck, put up their own tents and cook their own food. Welcome to the programme, Don.

Don: Thanks.

Mandy: This is a holiday with a difference, isn't it? Tell us, first of all, what sort of people go on a camping trip in Africa … and a long one at that … it is a month each trip?

Don: Yes. Well it sounds a sort of studenty thing to do, but in fact the majority of our passengers are people like doctors and lawyers. We do get some students but they tend to be the ones that are studying something like conservation or wildlife.

Mandy: And when do they all first meet?

Don: The evening before we set off. They fly in and I pick them up from the airport and immediately before we start sorting out places in the truck we go through what they've brought with them. Amazingly, every now and then we get somebody who genuinely doesn't realise it's a camping tour, so I have to rush out and get them blankets and a sleeping bag.

Mandy: It must be difficult – a whole group of strangers coming together and then having to live together like that.

Don: Mmm. It goes surprisingly well, but I always think the first day is critical because it sets the tone for the whole trip. We've had the odd nightmare start where we've got a flat tyre 20 minutes after we set off or it's dark and pouring with rain and people just can't get their tents up. Yeah, once we were making pasta late at night and the cook put in a tin of strawberry jam instead of tomato paste – those are the bad starts!

Mandy: Basically everyone has to take part in the domestic chores, do they?

Don: Yes. The brochure makes it clear that people have to work on a rota system and they usually do about an hour's work a day. We get a few who don't want to muck in but more often they are just untidy and I've got a bit of an eye for that because … well, they might leave a fork lying on the ground, for example, and okay, it's just a fork, but in a lot of places in Africa you can't get forks, so I'm quite possessive about the equipment.

Mandy: And do people really get on?

Don: A lot of people have never lived in a tight community situation like this before and you do get conflicts and personality clashes. The best approach is to observe it from afar. If it gets out of hand, I might point out in front of the whole group that there's a problem between certain people.

Mandy: Shame them a bit … .

Don: Mmm. Sometimes it works. To be fair, conflicts are rare but small problems *can* mount up in that kind of environment. Evening noise, for example. Some people want to go to sleep early and others don't. On occasions I've had to be the sort of go-between and impose a 'lights out' time if things start getting out of hand.

Mandy: What about getting up, because that's something we're really not keen on on holiday?

Don: If we're going into a wildlife park we might have to be on the road by six a.m. but people still ask why they have to get up so early. I've learnt how to do it now. If they're a quick group I'll get them up at five, but if they're slow I won't shout and scream at them – I just get them up at four thirty.

Mandy: Well, perhaps now we should go on to talk about what there is to see in some of those game parks that you have to get up so early for.

[pause]

Now you'll hear Part Four again.

tone

[The recording is repeated.]

[pause]

That's the end of Part Four.
There'll now be a pause of five minutes for you to copy your answers onto the separate answer sheet.

[Teacher, pause the recording here for five minutes. Remind your students when they have one minute left.]

That's the end of the test. Please stop now. Your supervisor will now collect all the question papers and answer sheets.
Goodbye.